GO WHERE THERE IS NO PATH

GO WHERE

WM
WILLIAM MORROW
An Imprint of HarperCollins*Publishers*

STORIES OF

HUSTLE,

GRIT,

SCHOLARSHIP,

AND FAITH

THERE IS NO PATH

Christopher Gray
with Mim Eichler Rivas

HarperCollins books may be purchased for educational, business, or sales promotional use. For information, please email the Special Markets Department at SPsales@harpercollins.com.

FIRST EDITION

Designed by Elina Cohen

Library of Congress Cataloging-in-Publication Data has been applied for.

ISBN 978-0-06-299209-3

21 22 23 24 25 LSC 10 9 8 7 6 5 4 3 2 1

TO EVERYONE WHO TAUGHT ME HOOD WISDOM—
FOR EMBODYING HUSTLE.

TO MY FICTIONAL AND REAL SUPERHEROES, ESPECIALLY
YOU WHO EMBODY BLACK EXCELLENCE—
FOR EXEMPLIFYING GRIT.

TO ALL TEACHERS, MENTORS, LIBRARIANS AND
WAY-SHOWERS WHO PRIORITIZE CRITICAL THINKING,
PROBLEM-SOLVING AND RESEARCH—FOR ELEVATING THE
VALUE OF SCHOLARSHIP.

TO ANYONE WHO HAS EVER SAILED INTO UNCHARTED
WATERS AND ALL WHO WILL IN THE FUTURE—
FOR PROVING THE POWER OF FAITH.

Do not go where the path may lead. Go instead where there is no path and leave a trail.

—Attributed to Ralph Waldo Emerson (1803–1882)

I will not follow where the path may lead but I will go where there is no path and I will leave a trail.

—Muriel Strode (1875–1964),
"Wind-Wafted Wild Flowers" (poem published August 1903)

Contents

Contents

GO WHERE THERE IS NO PATH

Introduction

A HERO can be anyone, even someone who makes a gesture as simple and reassuring as putting a coat around a young person's shoulder and letting that child know the world hasn't come to an end.

—Adapted from *Batman: The Dark Knight Rises*

This is the book I wish had been available to me back in the critical years of my youth. Born and raised in Birmingham, Alabama, the son of a single mom who had given birth to me when she was only fourteen years old, I believed wholeheartedly that the only way out of poverty and the systemic racism that impacted my community was through higher education. With excellent grades, scores, and recommendations, plus a strong leadership track record, I assumed that when the time came to apply to college and figure out how to afford it, the process would be readily presented to me. My job would be giving my all to follow that well-worn road.

Little did I know how wrong that assumption would be.

When the time came to pursue that set path, it was the middle of the 2008–2009 global economic meltdown, and not only had my mother lost her job but I now had two very young siblings who needed whatever financial resources we had left. Worse, without a penny of family income to help pay for college, I was also shocked to discover a messed-up financial aid system that was almost impossible to navigate for anyone struggling to afford higher education.

That was when I had to learn one of the hardest lessons of all, something I'd been taught by my great-grandmother, Big Ma: "When you can't find the way, you make a way."

Without telling me in so many words, my Big Ma prepared me to follow a path of my own making—or, in fact, to *Go Where There Is No Path.* Doing so changed my trajectory in dramatic fashion, making it possible both to afford college (and then some) and to use the priceless wisdom gained to become the CEO of my own tech start-up and social enterprise, which I launched at age twenty-two from my college dorm room.

Because there had been no book to guide me, I decided early in my journey that one day I'd have to write it myself so that others would find it easier to go forward. But given the demands of running a multimillion-dollar company that had grown exponentially in a very short period of time, that "one day" kept being postponed.

Part of my motivation to write this book came to me in moments when, against many odds, I was given opportunities that I could once only dream would be possible, and I had to wonder—*How did I even get here?* Whenever I encountered individuals struggling to chart their own success, I wanted to be able to answer their questions for me: *How did you do it?* And *How can I do it too?*

At the same time, I also wanted to respond to some of the skeptics who hear my story of becoming a social entrepreneur and wonder what it is about me that paved the way for my success, asking: *How did you really do it?*

Their implication is that when you grow up as an outsider without privilege, your success must be a fluke. An accident. It's either that or you got lucky. The inference is that if you grew up poor, are Black and gay, and come from a single-parent household and extended family where no one had ever gone to college, you are not legit. You get that look that says, *Hmmm, you must have worked the system*— aspiring to go to a top university and raking in scholarship money without access to a computer or the internet, and, later, invading the tech start-up space with no connection to the usual investment capital streams.

That thinking is old and it's painful. It's also taxing to be the face of your race or your income class or your sexuality and have to defend everyone who has ever been accused of "working the system."

The question also implies that, as a Millennial entrepreneur, you couldn't have paid your dues sufficiently to be able to hold your own at the important tables of power, privilege, and influence. There were times when I'd meet people so ready to dismiss the potential for success of those of us who grew up without means that it was just about like being asked, *Hey, how'd you rob that bank?*

Knowing how toxic that kind of dismissive treatment can be, I also wanted to share lessons I've learned for overcoming the odds with those of you who aspire to transform your circumstances, no matter where you are in your journey. I wanted to show you that *it can be done*.

By "it" I mean that success isn't a dragon you need to go slay to prove yourself worthy. I mean that whatever your qualifications or your pedigree, impressive or not, you get to determine where and how far you go, and how you will get there. What's more, I wanted to write this book to challenge those of you with competitive, entrepreneurial minds to look closely at social entrepreneurship. As someone who believes it's possible to build a for-profit company that offers real solutions to our most pressing social issues, I'm eager to recruit problem-solvers who want to contribute to our collective economic well-being as well as their own.

You know the old cliché about doing what you love and the money will follow? I'm not sure that's always true. But

I do believe that there are rewards to be gained from doing big things that bring about positive change in the world. In my experience, *if you lead with the good AND do the work*, the money will follow.

Some see social entrepreneurship as "conscious capitalism." I see it as smart business. When you enrich the lives of others, you enrich the marketplace for your products, services, and ideas.

That said, I know there's some confusion about what a social entrepreneur is. It isn't a career I grew up hoping to pursue one day. In my childhood, if you had asked me, "What do you want to be when you grow up?" I might have said, "Batman!" Let me correct that. What I really wanted to be was Bruce Wayne—making lots of money so I could afford to do lots of good. So maybe I always did want to do this.

The term "social entrepreneur" wasn't in common use for much of my life, and definitely not in Birmingham. In college, as a double major in finance and entrepreneurship, I was exposed to conversations early on about a new breed of tech start-ups that were beginning to tackle societal issues. I liked the concept that you could make money and make a difference, but no one was pointing me toward a path that would take me in that direction.

Naturally, that's because there was no such path.

In addition to hoping to be a voice of empowerment and practical advice to individuals of all ages eager to get their start-ups off the ground, I wanted to address the many misconceptions about what it takes to break into the tech world. Additionally, I had insights to share about why many start-ups fail. Historically, Silicon Valley investors have missed out on promising ventures because the entrepreneurs didn't get there on traditional paths. The rejection I encountered would later turn out to be a blessing—although I still hope to shake up the status quo of Silicon Valley.

My brief memo to the tech world would suggest rethinking the prevailing model of valuation. For too long, valuation has been tied to how much investment has been generated simply because some venture capitalists wrote big checks to a start-up. Now there is a new breed of young, visionary influencers and product creators and social entrepreneurs whom I'm happy to help represent. I'd urge the tech world to look at our revenue streams, our profitability, and our sustainability for better measures of valuation.

I clearly had a lot to say, but I have to admit it wasn't until early 2020 that I had the time to finally sit down and write. That's when the world suddenly changed, as you probably know well. The worldwide pandemic brought on by the novel coronavirus COVID-19 was a storm that invaded every aspect of our lives, and it was soon followed by a global economic collapse unlike anything any of us had seen before. All of that seemed to be the prologue for something even larger—a movement that rose up in a matter of days to confront not only the modern-day lynching of Black Americans by the police but to take on centuries of systemic racism and outright white supremacy.

Out of those crosscurrents I realized that though this book was something I originally wanted to write, *Go Where There Is No Path* was now something that I *had* to write. Even though we have seen the virus disproportionately impact communities of color and populations who are among the poorest and most marginalized, in reality, few individuals or groups are immune. Even after the most turbulent transfer of power after a presidential election in our history, and even with encouraging reasons for hope on the horizon, we still are left with widespread hardship and acute uncertainty.

There is so much more we all can do together. We all have to learn to lead with the good, and it will pay dividends if only we can see beyond needs alone. As an example, at the beginning of campus shutdowns one of my first concerns was for all the students who were living and eating on campuses and whose financial aid and scholarships were often restricted when school was not open. Many had nowhere to go or live when dorms and cafeterias shut down. That was once me. My company moved fast to roll out a Student Relief Fund that rushed $200 individual grants in cash assistance to students, grads, and parents in need. While too many waited for government checks, we offered essential financial help to buy groceries, health care supplies, and other necessities. This was one small step, but it shows that if we can find new ways of solving old problems, we will begin to address the bigger social ills of income injustice.

Without a doubt, the world is ever changing, and that's all the more reason, I believe, to tell my story right now.

Beyond the questions of how *I* did it and how *you* can too, these new realities have spurred me to ask a few more questions for this book. How will we do it? What will we learn when we get beyond the pandemic and back to classrooms and can reflect and ask ourselves: How did we look for opportunity in crisis to solve problems plaguing us all? (No pun intended.)

My premise is that we are all dealing with uncertainty, but we have God-given resources for making it through if we blaze our own trails. That's something I want to say to my own generation and the next in line, and to those who came before me.

Hope is alive. I'm proof.

Once upon a time I was a little kid with a crazy big dream of success that few people believed could be achieved. They almost convinced me they were right. That is, until I found out that at my fingertips was everything I needed for thriving as my own boss and as the CEO of my own start-up, the only official title I've ever held.

Conventional wisdom says you need money to make

money. But I say you don't, as long as you are willing to do the work and make the most of resources overlooked by others. That's hustle. You have to be willing to face hardship, disappointment, failure, competition, and the disbelief, cynicism, and even mockery of others. That's grit. You have to seek knowledge relentlessly and apply the wisdom you've learned. That's scholarship. And you have to believe in yourself and what I can only call a higher power to know that you *can* get to where you want to go even without a path. That's faith.

You have these resources. Everyone does. This book is for you as a reminder to put them to use for good. It's for audiences who are young or older, people of color, immigrants, those from diverse and mainstream backgrounds, LGBTQ+ or not, poor, middle-class, or privileged. Everything is possible for every single one of us. Everyone— that's who I'm writing for—but especially for anyone who can't see to the other side of their current crisis or can't see themselves represented in the arenas calling to them.

Uncertainty is not a life-threatening disease. I'm proof of that. Big, bold, world-shaking, massively profitable, and philanthropic ideas can in fact come out of bad times— even out of the worst times, when your natural instinct is to be afraid. We just don't have to *stay* afraid.

I used to think that we had a choice as to whether we went the traditional route or took the one that didn't yet exist. Now I believe we no longer have a choice, and that's not a bad thing. This book then is everyone's story, drawing from the toughest trials of our lives but spurring a movement that's creating greater opportunity for all.

Like my Big Ma told me, when we can't find the way, we'll make a way.

Chapter 1

Your Call to Action

Social entrepreneurs are not content just to give a fish or teach how to fish. They will not rest until they have revolutionized the fishing industry.

—**Bill Drayton, founder of Ashoka**

How did it feel?

That's a question I hear a lot from aspiring entrepreneurs who want to know how it felt to have the big aha! moment—the one that happens when you conceive of the idea that could be your version of winning the jackpot.

While I can't speak for everyone, I think that anytime you're struck by inspiration, it has a feeling of magic. To come up with an idea, then go from nothing more than a concept proposed by your imagination and turn it into something as massive as a multimillion- or billion-dollar enterprise—definitely that can be a heady experience.

It's no wonder that the most iconic tech wizards of recent years have been compared to superheroes with superhuman powers. The reality, however, is that for most entrepreneurs, tech and others, just having a killer, genius idea is no guarantee whatsoever that it's substantial enough to become a business, let alone a profitable one.

There is something to be said, though, about the added potential that appears when you've been attempting to solve a challenging problem and you rearrange the pieces of the maddening puzzle and suddenly you go "Oh!" And then you arrive at a fresh solution, that maybe no one's ever put together in the same way.

It's like the smoke clears and everything just clicks. I've heard researchers in the medical/tech space talk with almost a skeptical surprise about how those discoveries began. As in—*Huh, wait, did that just happen?* They repeat the experiment enough times to make sure the solution wasn't an outlier, sometimes getting a result for a problem they weren't even trying to solve. In fact, that's how antibiotics were accidentally discovered. Next thing they knew, history had been made.

I like imagining what Benjamin Franklin felt in his aha! moment, when he had a hunch that metal would conduct electricity and then went out to prove it with a kite and a key in a lightning storm. Or how Thomas Edison and his team felt, after so many failed attempts, when they finally came up with the right materials to carry an electric current and they flipped a switch and turned on the actual first light bulb. Franklin and Edison may not have had the full picture yet as to how their inventions would change life on Planet Earth for all of humanity, but they must have realized that they would not be lacking for customers for a very long while.

We've all had brainstorms—great ideas—and then second-guessed them. Maybe they weren't actionable. Or scalable. Or potentially profitable. Maybe we ran with them and they didn't go anywhere. Usually, I would add, when we lose traction on our own efforts it's because they don't have that same wow! feeling that entrepreneurs, inventors, and speculators like to recall about striking gold.

The best way to describe how my most dramatic aha! moment felt (there were earlier, lesser ones) was like a tap on the shoulder—as if the universe was trying to get my attention. When all you've been getting have been red lights, you suddenly get that tap. Like all systems are go. There's that path ahead, and you're not sure where it's going but you don't care—because you've got your own compass that's pushing you onward.

All of this is to try to answer the question. My hope is that it may be helpful to you at different times in your life when you're wondering which way to go—with an idea, an offer, or a decision, whenever you're contemplating your next step.

Those aha! moments—when it might seem that you've come to a clearing in the woods—are, to me, inflection points. They are peak moments that will change what happens next. And how that state has really felt in my experience is as a Call to Action.

If you ever have any of those feelings, all I want to say is—heed the call.

For me the big Call to Action came in the spring of 2013, in my third year at Drexel University in Philadelphia, just over six months after my twenty-first birthday. One of the reasons that I chose Drexel was for its LeBow Business School, a stellar program, where I could take classes as an undergrad. There was also the opportunity to add a fifth year off campus and intern in the field of my choice, earn college credit for it, and get paid. Turns out, just because you have a ton of scholarships and financial aid doesn't mean you can access dollars whenever you need them.

My co-op internship the first semester of my third year had been an eye-opening experience at Fannie Mae—where I saw firsthand why government-supported and -backed programs periodically falter even when intended for good. When I returned to campus, full of steam to take on the status quo and confront systemic issues, I found myself immediately busier than ever with my unofficial job helping friends, fellow students, and friends of friends find outside scholarship money and navigate the maze of the financial aid process.

Two and a half years earlier, in the fall of 2010, I had arrived in Philadelphia as a stranger in a strange land. My admissions offer had included a paid visit, and I had done almost a drive-by of Drexel and Philly. Everything, the buildings and the people, seemed to tower over me—and that's easy to do because I'm not the tallest person, although you wouldn't know it from my personality. Momma's five-foot-nine, and my father was over six feet. I say this having only one memory of meeting him when I was applying to college and he was required to sign my FAFSA paperwork.

Adjusting to the northeastern mentality wasn't easy. Once I got past my culture shock and started to make friends with students from a lot of different backgrounds, I kept hearing everyone talk about the continual struggle to get enough financial aid and about how to plan for dealing with mounting college debt from high-interest loans.

"Have you ever looked into applying for outside scholarships?" I'd ask, out of reflex—just as I had once done out of desperation. Very few knew anything about the shocking secret I'd come across after a similar suggestion had been made to me back in high school.

"Can you show me where to look?" I'd be asked, and then pretty soon I'd be demonstrating the various steps I took to track down scholarships. Word rapidly spread that I had this talent for finding obscure scholarships that were available not just for your first year of college but for the rest of your undergraduate and even graduate years.

As long as I had the time, I was eager to pass on everything I'd learned from the almost eight grueling months I'd spent in search of money for college when I was in high school. However, as junior year got underway at Drexel and I became more heavily involved in an outside project looking into venture capital possibilities and my course load became overwhelming, there wasn't enough time. My biggest disappointment was when a high school applicant I'd been helping with admissions didn't get accepted to her dream school. Her other options didn't offer the same amount of financial aid, and the only way to offset the cost was to go in search of outside scholarships. There wasn't much time. It had taken me continual hunting for more than half a year to get a list of possibilities that would fit my specific background, need, merit, and interests, and then to write the essays.

My sense of injustice was fired up. There had to be another, more expedient way to help students of color, students without resources for tutors or college test prep courses and, like the teenager I had been, without technology or the time to find and apply for potential scholarships.

Come to think of it, there had to be a better way to create more access to opportunity for every student.

That's close to what I said out loud to a fellow student as we headed back to the dorms late that March night of 2013: "There's gotta be a better way!"

She agreed. Where had I said that before?

If I had to choose a major antagonist and social ill that I've battled since childhood, it would be poverty—an evil aided and abetted by the thugs of racism, xenophobia, homophobia, violence in all forms, exploitation, ignorance, greed, injustice, oppression, inhumanity, threats to individual and environmental health, and more. The way I see it today, in order to solve a systemic problem that is as age-old and pervasive as poverty, solutions are most likely to be found by people who have lived the reality of the problem.

From an early age, I believed wholeheartedly that education was the one superpower that could successfully combat poverty. The best metaphor that I can give for growing up poor is being stuck on Shipwreck Island, as I named it, with limited radio reception. Nobody I could see ever seemed to make it off the island. In my mind, the only ship coming to get me out of there would arrive by the force of my own will to study and work above and beyond expectations. Self-education outside of school was necessary too, and so were efforts to improve myself in every way that I could. With all the intensity, optimism, and persistence that pretty much describe me, I faithfully believed that when the time came to apply for college, my ship would come in. It would carry me off to a top university out of state where I'd get a degree or two and land a rewarding career as a business executive and maybe a community leader of some sort.

College loomed in the distance like a lighthouse in the dark. If I could hold out, I knew my prayers to get off the island would at last be answered.

To my shock, in my junior year of high school, when the time did come to start my research about where to apply, I discovered that it wasn't as easy as all that. Just because you have excelled doesn't mean all doors will fly open and you can walk on in. The costs had become staggering, for one thing. Even public and state schools were costly. Another thing was that we were still living with the fallout from the economic crash of 2008–2009, made worse by a housing crisis in Birmingham.

Then my mother lost her job. Until my midteens, I had been the only child in our household, and Momma had always managed to hustle up enough work to support the two of us. When I was fifteen, my mother and a new man in her life had two babies in fast succession, and the new family dynamic brought about drastic changes for me. Being a big brother of two very young siblings gave me an added sense of responsibility. I'd always been independent, and now, the tougher things got, the more ready I was to get off the island.

There were stretches when we were basically homeless. To ease the load on my mother, I went to stay with my grandfather, who lived closer to my school. He was wonderful and supportive—except for when the subject of college came up. He couldn't relate, and so he couldn't understand why I had begun to worry that there would be no resources at all for me to attend college out of state. Around that point, it began to register with me why people don't follow any path at all—not the one that is unmarked, and not the one that's more delineated. Some people make do with where they are and just stay in one place.

Remember, you never have to apologize to family and friends who may resent your ambition or your dissatisfaction with how things are. You have to tune that static out. Don't listen to comments that make you feel bad because you're being all uppity for wanting to attain more education and create better opportunities for yourself. Even the people who love you the most may feel threatened. Though it's common in many families and communities, the resentment still hurts. On the flip side, I've heard from peers about being pushed too hard. Some were made to feel that if they didn't get accepted into the most exclusive Ivy League school, or recruited by the football team at the biggest D-1 university, or get perfect grades or test scores, they were some kind of a lost cause. Whether pushed too hard or not pushed enough, neither attitude is helpful.

What I learned eventually is that when you understand the application process—which I'll address further on—you will absolutely get into the right school for you. I promise. As for the lack of support at home you may experience, all I can say is that you will find your cheering squad if you are willing to look for real supporters.

The good news for me was that there was a great deal of encouragement at Ramsay High School, a highly ranked public magnet school that rewarded academic ambition and civic involvement. As a freshman at Ramsay, I attended an awards ceremony for graduating seniors and, for the first time, heard about the existence of outside scholarships—financial awards that are not institution-specific. After the ceremony I hurried over to ask one of the award recipients, out of great curiosity, "How did you apply for that scholarship? Did they find you?"

"No," he said with a laugh. Apparently, you could find a few outside scholarships online if you took the time to hunt for them. And then he gave me award-winning advice: "If you give it a try, don't wait till the last minute. Apply before you start your college applications."

His words stayed with me, thankfully.

In the fall of 2005, the year I started the ninth grade at Ramsay, I made one of the best decisions of my early life when I decided to call around the city and find out if there were any organizations or groups offering classes on managing money and starting businesses. In an instance of magical timing, I was told about the newly formed Community Entrepreneurship Institute, a nonprofit started by a woman who would turn out to be perhaps my most important mentor. Dr. Karen Starks—a social entrepreneur in her own right who was passionate about creating business and employment opportunities for urban residents—had recently started a teen empowerment program that met once a week at a downtown building known as the Innovation Depot.

Dr. Starks and I forged an immediate bond. Her passion was to develop the interests and abilities of young entrepreneurs in lower-income high schools and communities of color, while I was passionate about learning everything she could teach me. A petite, pretty African-American dynamo, Karen Starks had a PhD and was a true intellectual who was hyper-educated and worked as an assistant professor and psychologist on the faculty of the University of Alabama's School of Social Work. Most of the other kids in our teen group thought she was my mom. We resembled one another—she's shorter than me, unlike my mother, who is quite tall—but more than that, we spoke the same language. Dr. Starks probably understood better than anyone my preoccupation with going out of state to college. Once I started my junior year of high school, her advice was to begin thinking about where to apply to college by going online and taking virtual tours of campuses.

Dr. Starks said, "Make sure you check out what they've got to offer."

That advice helped me bear in mind that most colleges and universities are looking to attract great candidates. Even state-run schools and community colleges are marketing themselves. When you remember that you are shopping for a great school, that gives you leverage.

There was a hitch in my case, though, and one not uncommon for many living in poverty: my access to computers was limited. All I had was an old rickety desktop my grandfather kept, but there was no internet access at his house. When I could, I'd reserve a computer in the library at school, where I'd manage to get online briefly. There was also the Springville Road Public Library, where I had actually been given my first summer job and where I'd learned how to do research and find books and articles that no one else could. That's where I'd go after-hours to continue looking for colleges to explore. Unfortunately, times being hard, you'd have to wait for a long time in the line to use the few computers the library had. When it was busy, the library restricted users to only a half hour each. As best I could, I'd take a couple virtual tours and try to check out the rest of the college later on by going online with my smartphone.

All of the most competitive universities, like the Ivy

League schools that interested me, had expensive application fees. No one ever explained to me that most colleges and universities would waive those fees for anyone with financial need. Another challenge was that you had to wait until you got your admissions offer in your last semester of high school to find out how much financial aid might be included. Some institutions could afford to offer you a full ride—much like the athletes got—but you still had to qualify for admission. Some of the private colleges were closing in on costing $60,000 a year and that didn't include travel, living expenses during holidays, school supplies, medicine if needed, clothes and toiletries, and necessities for your dorm room. Most institutions couldn't afford to offer a full ride but would give you some help navigating the different loans that were available.

By the spring of junior year I started to really worry.

The more I looked at the process—the multiple forms with financial disclosures to prove your need—the more overwhelmed I became. My guidance counselor, helpful but overtaxed with the needs of all the juniors and seniors, suggested staying in-state, pointing out that the cost would be a lot less.

So much for getting off the island.

That was when I remembered the advice given to me a couple of years earlier about hunting around for some outside scholarships before applying to colleges. With no better ideas, I began to search for whatever scholarships

I could find online, again mostly making do with my old-fashioned smartphone.

At the time, I appreciated outside scholarships as an option, but finding them didn't seem earth-shatteringly important. Later, I would recognize that getting this information was itself a Call to Action that was subtly showing me a way to take charge of a process that seemed so out of my control.

Let me point out that whenever someone gives you valuable advice that's unlike other input you've been given, take it to heart. Maybe it won't be life-changing, but you never know who might be handing you your HOW. We hear a lot about the need to discover our WHY. On college apps and job applications and investment pitches, WHY comes in very handy—why this college is for you, why this job, why your start-up for whoever it is who's about to write a check. But HOW can be an even more important superpower. You want to go to college—HOW are you going to pay for it? HOW are you going to apply yourself and put your education to work? HOW asks questions like that.

Scouring the internet for anything remotely connected to a scholarship or help with paying for college, I saw again how messed up the system can be. Other than a few big-name scholarships, searching for lesser-known awards reminded me of looking for a needle in a haystack. There was information to be found online, but it was scattered all over and often outdated. Some of the offerings were scams. I'm not sure what possessed me, but I kept notes on those and started an archive of funding sources that didn't apply to me. In the back of my mind, I thought maybe someone else looking for money might be interested.

There were scholarship awards for puppeteers, for zombie apocalypse fans, for short people, tall people, and Swahili speakers, for young chefs who had the best recipes for Thanksgiving leftovers. The process was so slow. All the time I was doing scholarship searches and writing essays on my old smartphone, I kept saying to myself, *There's gotta be a better way.*

Then one evening on the computer in the public library, I stumbled across a notice from the sponsor of a scholarship that said they wouldn't award the money if the applicant didn't actually fit the guidelines. Did that mean there was unclaimed money out there? In fact, it did. That night I began to index just how much. Soon I'd achieve an estimate that every year *millions* of dollars in awards go unclaimed.

How come nobody ever talked about this, given all the students looking for money and all this money looking for students? Somehow I had uncovered this crazy mismatch!

Again, I couldn't shake the thought that there had to be a better way.

In March 2013, as I said those words while walking back to my dorm—after late hours working in the computer lab on a start-up that I'd founded a few months earlier—my Call to Action echoed from years before. This time it could not be ignored. The truth is that I was mad. Families shouldn't have to go broke sending their children to college. Students shouldn't have to rely on loans with ballooning interest rates that they'll be forced to spend their early working years paying off. And that's *before* they can buy homes or figure out how to educate the children they hope to raise. I was mad that once you pinched your pennies to pay for your first year at college, you still had three more years to go, not to mention navigating the even harder to find financial aid for graduate school.

Two thoughts collided at the same time: Why wasn't there enough time for me to offer free workshops to help my fellow students do their scholarship research? And why wasn't there one central clearinghouse for all these different scholarships, a place that could match every award's specific criteria with an applicant's specific criteria?

Hit by these simultaneous thoughts, all at once I stopped in my tracks with a solution in hand to my old refrain of "there has to be a better way." There it was—a start-up idea that made all the sense in the world.

At these inflection points in my life, these aha! moments, once I see it and own it there's no turning back. That's what happened. First I got mad, right before the solution appeared, and then I took action.

No one could question whether or not this was the right

idea to take on immediately as an entrepreneur. It was in motion from the moment I stopped in my tracks. If you look at many of the business and social enterprises that achieve a good deal of success, you see there are two things they all seem to have in common: they all offer a novel solution to a problem, and they were inspired by the entrepreneur's own personal experience.

In solving a widespread issue, based on a personal challenge I had lived through, I had asked myself: *How do I help bring that solution to more people?* In the process, I saw there could be financial benefits to doing that. Helping others could be turned into a business. The old-school term says it well—a win-win. Or leading with the good and letting the money follow.

In the time just after your Call to Action moment, I would caution you about how many people you're going to tell about your undertaking, especially when the project is in its infancy. Maybe you have a lot of knowledge about the process of turning an idea into a reality. Maybe you have studied and read up all about how to get your brainstorm built and off the ground in a short amount of time. That will all be helpful. More than that, though, there are strategies for being successful after veering off the same path everyone else is on, and they may serve you even more.

And some of them you learned when you were young.

Chapter 2

When Life Tells You No, Tell Yourself Yes

I have learned that as long as I hold fast to my beliefs and values—and follow my own moral compass—then the only expectations I need to live up to are my own.

—Michelle Obama

Only recently have I begun to appreciate how much the battles of my growing-up years helped me find the inner strengths that I was eventually able to put to use—not only on a personal level but also in business. Now, you might wonder if this means that achieving success requires you to have had a difficult childhood or tough odds you had to overcome. But that's not my point.

My point is, we all have our own inner strengths that sometimes emerge earlier in our development when we do face challenges. They also emerge when we are loved, nurtured, guided, and empowered—often by parents and caretakers but also by educators, coaches, and guides who may come in a variety of forms. The strengths I'm talking about are not all lofty attributes. We all have them. Some are the things that make you different, that give you an edge, that get you worked up, that put a fire into you. They serve you in the long haul as the kind of resources that help you to define yourself—that help you to *tell yourself YES when life tells you NO.*

That one survival strategy allowed me to overcome bullies, racists, homophobes, and many (though not all) of the self-negating messages that being poor can level at you. Everyone it seems has asked me where that ability to rise above the noise came from. Not everything is learned. Some traits are just inherent. I've been able to rise above it all since I was little—in part because I'm talkative, animated, and innately able to remove myself from cross fire.

Though it's often said in other ways, and I can't say it enough, *belief in yourself is gold.* It's power. It makes others listen and can be disarming. Self-belief, when you do the work that leads to self-knowledge, informs your values, helps you separate right from wrong, and sets your moral compass.

Where do you find this gold? How do you get it to work for you? Can you keep it even when circumstances go south, whatever your stage of life?

Well, one of the first things you do to acquire and keep a belief in yourself is to *actively look for and prize it*. Begin with your story.

From the start, I was different. For better and worse.

My parents were both in their teens but not together that clear Halloween night in 1991 when I came screaming into life. A fighter mentality helped me survive a difficult birth and put that stamp on me from day one. My mother, Regina Gray, was a fighter too, and only fourteen when I was born—basically a child herself.

Often, over my early years, my mother was more of a big sister than a mom. Loving and protective, fun, moody, sometimes challenging, Momma did the best she could and worked hard to keep us fed, housed, and clothed. Even so, in certain respects I had to learn to mostly raise myself. Before I started school, I'd taught myself to read, to reason at a fairly adult level, and to fuel my own intellectual curiosity.

I'm sure that my biological father visited me when I was very young, but I have no memory of it. Otherwise, except for the time that we had to meet in my teens for him to sign my FAFSA paperwork, I had zero contact with him. When we sat down and I handed him the signature page, I waited to feel something. But there was no bond, no recognition from him that I was his son, and nothing in me that needed him to be daddy-like. I could have received his lack of interest in me—or discomfort—as a NO. As in, *No, you're not important to me.* But by then I didn't need his affirmation. My habit of telling myself YES was ingrained. I thanked him for his trouble, and we parted ways, for good. Instead of feeling a sense of loss for myself, I felt bad for him.

That's how much I believed in myself. My future was all ahead of me and I was going to do great things that he wouldn't be able to share in, that he wouldn't be able to claim he had helped shape. After seeing him, my fighter mentality kicked in even more. Not against him. After all, I couldn't be mad at someone who wasn't a presence in my life. Even so, I had a lingering question. *Why* wasn't he in my life? Strange as it sounds, I wanted to know what the social and psychological causes were that contributed to teens giving birth to children they couldn't raise.

No one around me seemed to be asking similar questions. So I kept them to myself and went in search of answers on my own.

On the positive side of things, my step-grandfather—who had been with my grandma (although they weren't together anymore)—had stepped up early in my life as the male and father figure that I needed. He was salt-of-the-earth, unpretentious, and as unselfish as the day is long. Some would say he was generous to a fault. That wasn't true in my opinion. Actually, he pinched pennies, owned a house, kept to a budget. Anything basic I learned about financial literacy came from him.

It wasn't until middle school that I heard the term at an assembly. A local African-American businessman wanted to engage middle and high school students of color on the subject and came to speak at an assembly. After he spoke, my curiosity was piqued enough that I asked the librarian at Springville Public Library how I could find out more about the topic.

"Financial literacy?" she asked, half-impressed, half-surprised that the subject was of interest to someone who looked so young to her. I was twelve or thirteen, not that young.

The librarian brought out a stack of books, and I chose one, for starters. It was somewhat general, but expanded my knowledge to concepts I would have never known about. As I read, it occurred to me that it had been written for people who had such things as savings and who'd never been late on bills or maxed out on credit cards. The truth was that my grandfather's approach—common sense—at least got me to thinking about the idea of earning more than you spend.

Where my grandfather did get extravagant was with us kids—my cousins and me. We were his priority, and it gave him joy to spend his hard-earned money on us. Rarely would he show up without toys and treats to surprise or entertain us; that didn't cost him a lot, but it did involve planning and knowledge of our likes and dislikes. Other adults would complain about him spoiling us, but he was someone who didn't feel he had to explain himself to the world. He was an early example of telling himself YES when the world said NO.

My mother's grandmother—my great-grandmother, Big Ma—embodied that same attitude and took it further, impressing it upon me. Every word from her to me was a form of YES. Her most common refrain, "Baby, you got to work for what you want," was how she lived her life. Nobody could keep her down.

My Big Ma made me believe that not only could I work hard but I had something special and important to give to the world. And if I did work hard and applied myself, she assured me, life would be good, because that was God's plan all along. In her eyes, I could do no wrong. In my eyes, she was a reflection of goodness and innate wisdom—despite her lack of an education—so I took her belief in me to heart. Her spirit of optimism shaped my values and got me to look at problems outside of myself and to try to make sense of them.

As I recall my childhood, I remember observing facets of life that I didn't yet understand but knew weren't right. Being poor in the 1990s in Birmingham, Alabama, was not easy, but it wasn't felt as acutely as it would be a decade later. Eventually, as I studied the causes and effects of poverty, I came to the conclusion that most people who are poor don't label themselves as such. Teens growing up around the country today typically don't see the systemic failures that cause their families to fall through the cracks so that they're barely making it, if at all.

Statistically speaking, poverty fell by almost half in Birmingham between 1990 and 1999. Generally, that was because the economy of the Clinton years was humming along and there were jobs to be had. But if a median annual income in those years was $30,000, you could be earning just above the poverty line of approximately $17,000 and that was not considered poverty. That would change, of course, during the 2000s, when "trickle-down" economics failed to trickle down and there was no work.

When money is short, you move a lot. You go from having a small bedroom of your own in housing that's approved by Section 8 zoning to a more crowded situation where you sleep on a sofa. You don't necessarily eat breakfast before you go to school, and generally, you have fewer vegetables and fruit and eat more meals that can be bought in bulk and more snack foods and candy that are less costly and more caloric. You might go from having brand-new clothes bought on discount to dreaded hand-me-downs. The downward shift is subtle. You never think that you're really poor like the rural folks, Black or white, in raggedy clothes and dirty faces, but you feel a sense of pressure—from the weight of adults trying to figure out how to pay rent, or from having utilities, cable, the phone, or water cut off.

Meanwhile, you're just trying to be a kid.

When you don't even have the words to name your condition, it's harder to fend off others' attempts to define you. Without education and the critical thinking needed to process how things got to be the way they are, you may assume you have no choice, no power to change anything. You start to question how education could possibly make a difference.

In our extended family, again, nobody I knew received an education past high school. Some didn't make it even that far. When I was growing up, Birmingham's inner-city neighborhoods followed many disturbing national trends. Now and then elected leaders would try to stem the tide, but the cycle remained: crumbling and underfunded public schools, rising numbers of high school dropouts, and worsening joblessness, plus the increasing presence and influence of gangs and drugs.

Even before I became familiar with the violent history of racism in Alabama—a state frequently named the most racist in the United States, with Birmingham deemed the most segregated of any urban city—I felt the impact of institutionalized discrimination. In the Deep South, bigotry has long been out in the open. Naively, I once thought racists only lived south of the Mason-Dixon Line, but I later found out that they live everywhere. Apparently—outside of those states that actually seceded from the Union during the Civil War, bias is sometimes more covert, more subtle. We would learn (as we have in these recent turbulent times) how pervasive and violent the hate has grown, especially when inflamed by the rhetoric of "normalized" white supremacy and that of "Us versus Them."

When you don't grow up in privilege, sooner or later you will experience the toll taken by the dual devils of poverty and inequality. In my own backyard, I witnessed a disproportionate rate of incarceration for people of color; I saw in my own family how the lack of access to legal assistance sent Black folks to jail for lesser offenses than the crimes committed by the privileged and connected who never saw the inside of a jail cell.

By the time I graduated from college, the prison system would increasingly be described as the "new Jim Crow." By then I understood that, according to the Federal Bureau of Justice Statistics, one in three African-American men can expect to be incarcerated—compared to the one in thirty-one Americans in the general population who get caught up in various phases of the criminal justice system. Another significant statistic about incarcerated adults is that 70 percent of inmates can't read at even a fourth-grade level—another reason why we have to advocate for greater investment in public education and literacy programs.

In Birmingham, Black neighborhoods suffered all the

more from a housing crisis that began to percolate in the early 2000s and would explode at the same time as the Great Recession skyrocketed joblessness, impacting every adult I knew.

You don't grow up in the hood in the Deep South without a passing knowledge of the ills of poverty and racism, even if you haven't decided you're supposed to come up with solutions. In all honesty, though, I wasn't always focused on fighting racial oppression. Some days I was just trying to dodge a more garden-variety kind of onslaught common in many zip codes: name-calling and bullying.

Bullies come in all forms. Sometimes they don't look like the cartoon version of bullies. Sometimes they're folks you know who seem wired to diminish your confidence with subtle micro-aggressions; sometimes they use outright threats, physical abuse, or violence to instill fear in you. Maybe you are not the intended target but you happened to be there, wherever that was—on the street, in the neighborhood, even at family gatherings.

In my memories, there was often an escalation moment in many of those settings when disses could become taunts, or out of the blue somebody somewhere had to say something that would lead to an exchange of harsh words. Most of the time I stayed out of the fray. I was a bookish bigmouthed kid who could talk back at times, so I had to learn to thicken up my skin if the remarks were sent my way. It was much harder when someone else without defenses was being bullied, including adults targeted by other adults. My edge was sometimes to remember that when the swipes were aimed at me it was only someone foolish trying to tell me NO to make themselves feel more superior.

My YES to myself was a challenge to my inner stamina to not let them win. If needed, I could adopt an emotional coldness that let me detach quickly from situations. Later, that reflex definitely helped me learn how to deescalate work conflicts and other situations. Understanding the potential for people to just go off all of a sudden taught me to be an astute reader of others and their moods. In sales, marketing, and leadership, that can be a lasting street skill.

School bullies were a lot more predictable. Look, if you're a nerd who makes all As and sometimes is the teacher's pet, as I was, they'll find you. The usual bullies would assume that I'd be easy prey. Being small, I'm sure they didn't see me as someone who could fight back. But I could. My mother made sure of that. At the least, I could run faster than any of them just to stay out of the fray. But Momma was adamant that I not show weakness. To this day, I still resist showing any hint of intimidation, even when I feel it—which can be counterproductive. However, I did learn to fight strategically. Sometimes I could negotiate my way out of getting my ass kicked. Other times, with a sharp tongue, I could psyche out my tormentor before any blows fell. Or, when push came to shove—literally—I would pit two bullies against each other, sit back, and let them have at it.

Knowing I stood almost no chance of physically winning in a brawl, I chose to learn to outsmart the opposition. It took me a while to learn how powerful that can be.

If given a choice as to what I would change about how I grew up, there would be a few things. The experience of being bullied is one of them, definitely. Some strengths did emerge from it, though. In a business context today, I seek higher ground for negotiations, where everyone can walk away with something gained. Whenever I see young people being bullied—or taken advantage of—I take action. Part of that does come from having been in their shoes.

Mixed messages confused me as a kid. On the one hand, I was expected to fight and not back down or show fear. On the other, I worried that any trouble—especially trouble that got me sent to the principal's office—would leave a lasting stain on my record, enough to derail my plans and goals. Sometimes it was hard to balance expectations that I should maintain my straight-A student reputation while also flexing my influence by winning fights. Ultimately, in weighing both messages, I chose self-belief and told myself YES by deciding I wasn't going to sabotage my future.

As none of the adults around me seemed to be an expert

at deescalating fights, the challenge eventually was to teach myself to do so—to play out the situation and discern what the best line of action was going to be.

When you choose to look back at your life and examine how you made decisions for yourself, you'll most likely find that you had your own moral compass all along. You'll probably also realize how often you told yourself YES when the world said NO.

The main lesson I want to share with you is that the fight for self-belief is always more readily won when we search for knowledge to help us decipher right from wrong. Sometimes that knowledge comes from inherent sensibilities that give us tremendous guidance for small and large decisions. There are times, however, when we need to seek outside input. For me, that came from a range of sources, and also from being an insatiable reader.

In the world that shaped me, I didn't take people and things at face value. Trust was not always a given. So I looked to books and other outlets to at least give me another perspective. Scholarship was never an imposition; it was empowering. Reading was my refuge, my saving grace, my early therapy. If there was ever something I needed to understand, I'd check out a book from the library. Over the years I read everything from biographies of notable leaders and entrepreneurs to books on psychology, family dysfunction, and socioeconomic influences impacting youth like me growing up in the inner city.

One day when I was in the seventh grade, someone made a statement about something being a sin—according to what the preacher said—and I asked, "Where does it say that in the Bible?" The person who said that hadn't read any Scripture but relied on the authority of the preacher, without question.

That little exchange prompted me to borrow a Bible and read it for myself. No one in my family, to my knowledge, had read it. Other than now and then, we didn't go to church on a regular basis. That didn't keep anyone from professing to know what Jesus meant or said—but that was all the more reason to search for answers from the book itself.

For the next several years of my life, the Bible became my bible—for lack of a better term—that empowered me with everything I needed to say YES to myself when the world told me NO. As I think about it today, the seeds for one day becoming a social entrepreneur were planted in me from the moment I read the Bible all the way through.

Organized religion would be something I'd question over the years. Yet that had nothing to do with my personal faith, my self-belief, and my search for a moral compass. Reading both the Old and New Testaments, I faithfully embraced the premise that we're all created to be fruitful and to prosper. That was reassuring, especially at that age when fitting in socially matters so much, and when I wanted a code of moral behavior to follow. In James 2:14–26, I learned something that opened my eyes. James says, "What good is it, my brothers, if someone says he has faith but does not have works?" (English Standard Version). He goes on to say that without works, faith is dead.

That teaching struck a chord with me and became a lasting value. Like that old-school saying—you have to walk the walk, not just talk the talk. The lesson was clear that sometimes it's better not to talk the talk at all, but just to let your actions speak for themselves.

The biblical teachings that felt ready-made to change my life came from Solomon the Wise. A king of Israel, Solomon was one of the earliest examples of an entrepreneur I'd ever encountered—hundreds of years BC. As the successor to his father, King David, Solomon saw unrest and poverty in the kingdom and came up with a number of solutions— including the creation of many new trade routes and the development of a monetary system that put more money into the hands of more people in the land.

The story that grabbed me was of a dream Solomon had early in his reign. In it God spoke to Solomon and asked him what he most wanted. Solomon asked for wisdom and knowledge so that he would have "an understanding mind to govern your people, that I may discern between good and evil" (1 Kings 3:9, English Standard Version). The Lord was so pleased with his response that, in addition to wisdom and knowledge, he promised Solomon "riches, possessions, and honor, such as none of the kings had who were before you, and none after you shall have the like" (2 Chronicles 1:12, English Standard Version).

King Solomon used his wisdom to lead the nation of Israel into its golden age of wealth, expansion, and influence. He ruled benevolently, avoiding war and forging peaceful alliances with neighbors like Egypt and Arabia. He wrote love poems, gave advice, held court to decide difficult cases (his decisions would later influence laws around the world), and was accessible to people from every walk of life. Whenever foreign royalty came to visit, it was Solomon's wisdom, not his wealth or his power, that they most admired. Allegedly, he had every love interest he could ask for—including the Queen of Sheba.

It may sound presumptuous for a teenage boy growing up in Birmingham, Alabama, to have aspired to be like Solomon—thousands of years after he lived and ruled until the ripe old age of eighty. But I did. Whenever I was going through a rough stretch, I'd pray for wisdom. Even these days, one of the most challenging periods in the history of our country, I pray for wisdom, as Solomon did.

The wisdom lived deep inside of me. My prayer was to be guided to it. Knowledge helped to supplement that wisdom. In academics as in business, having an in-depth command of the knowledge in your field is essential. Information remains the coin of the realm. Still, there is no substitute for the wisdom that gives us a code of right action to live by.

What a gift. For most of high school, I was rarely without my Bible. It was a reminder not to feel sorry for myself, no matter what. Even when things got much harder for my family and me, self-pity was never an option. Self-belief was the only option.

Over the years I've encouraged friends and employees—including those who are older than me—that when charting out their next moves, they should look to their own wisdom, their own inner guidance. We all have it.

When you choose to express your wisdom, even when it goes against the grain, that's another form of telling yourself YES when the world has said NO.

Listening to my wiser side, over time I began to accept that the bullies and haters were never going to change. When I ran this awareness by Dr. Starks, she agreed, explaining that those who grow up in a certain environment adapt by acting and thinking like everyone else around them. For many it's survival. Education and literacy, in her view, were critical for empowering and helping those people develop their own mindsets.

Being told that you can't do something happens in all communities. Your ability to brush off those limits, she explained, is about finding your own drive—call it self-motivation. That is the key for anyone to truly thrive.

My translation of Dr. Starks's wisdom was to more

thoughtfully choose the words that I spoke to myself in my head. A lot of people, regardless of socioeconomic background, wind up with a mindset of self-deprecation and even inferiority, often as an echo of how others speak to them or how they speak to themselves. If you grow up hearing racists calling you or your parents or family members the most derogatory, debasing names, you have to mount a big internal offense to refuse to take on those attributes. You have to guard your moral compass so it can filter out the negative messages—whether aimed at you or at others.

For example, there was an episode I can clearly recall from my early adolescence that took place at a family gathering. Some of the adult members started saying terrible things about a distant cousin of mine, who plainly had some learning disability issues.

Instead of showing empathy or concern for a family member, the adults, male and female, began to ridicule him for being overweight and for his effeminate mannerisms. "Well, only one way to fix that," one of the men said. "You need to beat the gay out of him." The answer that came back was "Oh, well, we've already done that," but it hadn't "took" yet.

My own coming out and even any awareness of sexuality wouldn't happen until much later, when I was in college. Even so, I was outraged and let it be known, telling them, "Y'all don't see that he has some developmental problems?" I pointed out that he was in special education and was already being bullied. Maybe a professional could help with behavioral issues, I suggested, way more than being beaten. My comments were not warmly received.

The good news at least was that I had learned to use my voice, and that was no small thing. No matter what stage of the journey you're at, check your moral compass regularly; it points you toward the use of your voice and toward right action for yourself and for others. You don't have to lose your fighter mentality either, as long as you know what's worth fighting for and what's not. The more you learn to trust your own judgment and your own belief in right versus wrong, and the more you own up to your situation, without blame or self-pity, the more empowered you will feel.

When you begin to rely on your own values and reject the limiting attitudes and behavior of peers, family members, or outsiders that don't feel right to you, it can be one of the most liberating feelings in the world. That's when you start to really strengthen and grow and prepare yourself for charting an exciting future.

We tend to focus on all the skills needed for success while we might want to focus *less* on our *skillset* and *more* on the *mindset* for success. This is relevant whether you're getting ready to apply to college, pursue professional opportunities, pitch a start-up to investors, or generally prepare to venture out into uncharted territory.

Cultivating a mindset for success is the ultimate in saying YES to yourself no matter how loudly the world tells you NO. My top suggestion for cultivating that mindset for success is to do an inventory of your goals and values. You might start with some of the things you were told you couldn't do and then replace those NOs with all the things you know you *can* do. When you set your sights on a goal, despite any direct path toward it, and declare that you *can* and that you *will* get there, that can give you powerful drive. When you give voice to a moral value by putting into writing what you *believe* in, the words you choose to use on the page will serve as wise road signs that help you stay focused on your goals.

Without a doubt, wisdom comes in different forms and different styles. So too do other traits you can put to use for yourself—if you're ready to hustle, the subject of the next chapter.

Chapter 3

Hustle and the Art of Being Resourceful

I am a hustler, baby; I sell water to a well.

—Jay-Z

Rarely do I read or hear a great entrepreneurial saga that does not emphasize the importance of hustle in some shape or form. In fact, its mention has become so ubiquitous that I've heard my tech and start-up peers try to downplay it. Their attitude is like, *Tell us something we don't know.* On the flip side, in some business circles hustle is talked about so reverentially, you'd think that's all you need.

The debate intensifies when you start to pay attention to the different contexts for how people use the term "hustle"—and also "hustler." Those words have so many associations that they've become stand-ins for a whole catalog of things. For example, if you look up "hustle" in the Urban Dictionary, you'll find at least six different definitions, starting with (1) the current, more common usage that says you need to be bold and confident to go out and grind so you can make it in the urban jungle of whatever you are pursuing. "Hustle" can also allude to (2) an intense focus on earning lots of money in general, and sometimes specifically (3) through shadier avenues of street business—for instance, as a pimp or prostitute, or selling drugs, or small-time forms of gambling. Sometimes you might have a legit job but to get by you need to add either a (4) side hustle that may or may not be legit too, or a (5) side hustle that can be a pet project you do in your spare time that you think could be your main hustle one day. And apparently (6) there was a disco dance in the '70s called "the Hustle." If you Google it, you'll find there was even a song called "Do the Hustle."

As if all that's not enough, "hustle" can just mean to hurry up and not waste time at getting things done. A "hustler" can have swag and charisma to an admirable degree and is typically a superior salesman who can sell you the shirt off your own back. But "hustler" does have a questionable vibe to it—whether it's used to refer to a drug dealer who gets you hooked on their product or a con man or woman trying to sell you on something you don't need or want, or trying to run a hustle ("a con job") by you. Or a "hustler" can just be someone who is unapologetic about

playing to win, no matter the situation, someone who believes, "Ain't no shame in the game."

For some people, hard work and hustle are not a
choice but really their only options for survival. Most of
us are familiar with the various connotations. Yet when I
go back to the lessons I learned growing up in the hood,
there is another understanding of "hustle" that often goes
underappreciated—*the art of being resourceful.*

That brand of hustle seemed to flourish all around me.
All the women in my family—my mother, my aunt, my
grandmother and great-grandmother—had that classic
ability to "make a silk purse out of a sow's ear." Maybe that's
why it took me until the age of eight to even realize how
hard Momma had to hustle. As my consciousness developed, I began to better appreciate all the obstacles overcome by African-Americans throughout our history and
how the art of resourcefulness had allowed us, individually
and collectively, to "make a way out of no way."

In our extended family and in the neighborhood, I saw
many different examples of the resourcefulness of hustlers. Some were legit and others were street entrepreneurs
whose businesses were not. From my study of the Bible
and in my search for wisdom, I agreed with the Scripture
that stated: "Judge not that ye be not judged." That being
said, as time went on it was obvious to all that crime was
only going to pay in the short run. There's a reason that you
don't see many older drug dealers—because sooner rather

than later most wind up dead or in jail. Meanwhile, I often think about how successful some of the street hustlers would have been if they had managed to combine their street-bred marketing skills with an actual business school education.

No one really wants to deal drugs, in my view. But when entire industries go by the wayside, where are people supposed to go for work? This was an issue I observed growing up but it hadn't always been that way in my hometown. In the late nineteenth century, Birmingham, the largest city in Alabama—seen as the state's industrial crown jewel—became known as the Magic City because of its railway connectivity. For the next century, they used to say that if you didn't want to migrate to the Northern and Midwestern cities for opportunities, you could always find employment in Birmingham, which became a magnet for rural African-American workers and poor Irish and Italian immigrants. Jobs were plentiful at the area's mining operations, steel mills, and ironworks, along with factories engaged in manufacturing and building for railroad and transportation businesses. In fact, one of Birmingham's great claims to fame as the Magic City was that within a mere ten-mile radius were all the natural resources needed for making iron—limestone, coal, and iron ore.

So part of Birmingham's origin story included that spirit of industry, connectivity, energy, and hustle. All of that came to a grinding halt during the Great Depression, making the Magic City suddenly one of the poorest of the bigger cities in the country. But with the onset of World War II and the urgent demands of the war effort, the city once again became an industrial leader, and factory and mining jobs became plentiful again.

Up through the 1970s, those jobs could still sustain communities and provide steady employment, medical insurance, and even some retirement benefits; families could afford to buy modest homes, send their kids to college, *and* save money for retirement. But other trends had soured the magic. As the most segregated city in the Deep South and the most adamantly anti-union, Birmingham saw wages stagnate as opportunities for blue-collar work declined. Once the steel mills closed for good and trains stopped being a key mode for transporting goods, the new banking and telecommunications businesses wanted more educated workers. The problems were local but were made worse whenever there was a national economic downturn—with waves of people out of work.

This was the backdrop to many people's choice to earn a living any way they could. Hustle was survival.

No matter what time period we're talking about, and no matter what your regular hustle (or side hustle) was or is, if you came up on the streets, you were learning the fundamentals of "hood wisdom." Most everyone who grows up in that environment manages to pick up the main elements. Hood wisdom has its own code of ethics. It comes with a confidence, a love of competition, a relentlessness, and, sometimes, a cutting tongue. Your resources are your fast wit, a hard work ethic, and an ability to be a quick study. You learn to observe, listen, and pay attention to trends. To have wisdom in the hood, you have to follow your gut on decisions, you have to fine-tune your instincts, and you have to read people well.

A lot of the lessons that lead to hood wisdom apply to smart business practices in general—such as: *the customer is always right, be first to market, be innovative,* and *your reputation will precede you.* You learn that *if you have to pay someone to do something for you, make sure you know their job inside and out so you're aware of what they are supposed to be doing.*

Hustlers with hood wisdom are often practical, realistic, fatalistic, and tough. In the hood, if someone lets you down or plays you, it would be unwise to give them another chance. Then again, if you part ways with someone, you don't want to burn a bridge—or, at least, you don't want to scorch it down to the ground completely if you plan on crossing that bridge again someday.

One aspect of hood wisdom that I learned to appreciate even more over time is the notion that if you don't make things happen on your own by creating opportunities for yourself—no matter what the channels—you will be left behind. And again, the thing that people overlook about hustle is that being forced to create your own opportuni-

GO WHERE THERE IS NO PATH

ties is the basic training for learning to make a way out of no way.

The thing I later heard frequently from scholarship review boards and from admissions officers was not necessarily that they were impressed with my hustle. The word they used was "initiative." Their point was to acknowledge the initiative I'd demonstrated, for example, by scouting around to find out if there were any local organizations teaching youth about financial literacy and entrepreneurship—which led to my creation of a for-profit business and a nonprofit philanthropy while I was still in high school. Later on, when I was just trying to get my business off the ground and there was no budget to hire marketing experts or PR professionals, I hustled over to my college's communications department and was given a free crash course in how to stage my own press conference and gain media exposure quickly. That turned out to be about as close to hitting the jackpot as possible, so much so that I almost wasn't prepared to accommodate the exposure that first press conference generated all at once.

My point is that you don't have to come from the hood to apply the principles of street entrepreneurship. They're simple. Sometimes you may actually be surprised by your own hustle—or initiative, if you prefer—when you *initiate action toward a meaningful goal*. Instead of being intimidated by competition for resources and opportunities, you hustle to get there first. You ask questions, you knock on doors, and you take time to research and develop a plan on your own. You aren't waiting for someone to inform you of opportunities or to lead you to them. You are DIY with your future success.

Hustle can get you everywhere.

Hustle can also be your best teacher. My bet is that you may well have used it to your advantage in the past, or have it within you but have never needed to seriously activate it. For me it was a necessity, starting at around the age of eight, when I got a crash course in hustle after I was told "no."

Regina Gray, my mom, had a competitive streak that was guided by survival. Her hood wisdom was a playbook for using inner resources. She was smart, outgoing, and tough. If her lack of formal education stood in the way of getting a better-paying position, Momma would still work the job she hated but then enroll in a night class to learn book-keeping. At one point, she used those skills to start her own business helping other small businesses with their books. I watched and learned from that. In hustler fashion, Regina Gray could also stretch a dollar as far as it could go and hide the fact that we didn't have much. Rarely would she complain or put up with self-pity—not from herself and not from me. As for hood wisdom, I saw her use her charm and her toughness. There were limits. Her stumbling block, I felt, was that even though she was worldly and could read people well, somehow that didn't extend to the men in her life.

Between Momma, her momma, and Big Ma, the women in my family reached deep into their pockets if need be to make sure that I didn't have to go without anything of importance. If I asked my mother for something I really wanted, the competitive side of her would kick in and she'd try to get it for me without asking anyone else to help. When I was in the third grade, however, the thing I wanted did in fact push the limit.

"You want—*what?*" Momma asked after I'd mentioned the latest Nintendo Pokémon video game that I was dying to have.

To this day I maintain that as important as literacy is, so too are all the forms of multimedia children consume— despite some of the negative side effects. Video games, for a child with as much energy and as short an attention span as me, were lifelines to other worlds. If I wasn't going to sit quietly and read, I could actively throw myself into the virtual reality of a video game where lessons of hustle and codes of ethical behavior could be learned. Game-controllers that let you physically engage with that world made you feel powerful when life was making you feel otherwise.

Video-game content developers actually seeded important messages and dialogue into the games, giving heroic attributes to many of the characters who had to face off against evil or mischief-making. The Pokémon phenomenon offered an array of "pocket monsters" with various powers and weaknesses, an interesting way to teach players to identify those traits in themselves too. My favorite was Rapidash, the unicorn who could cause wildfire, and that pretty much explains how I saw myself as different even then.

After Momma found out how much the game would cost, almost $50, for the first time ever she told me flat out, "Christopher, you know we don't have that kind of money." She wasn't being mean, but the time had come to get real.

Did I know that? Had she been spoiling me all along? Had something happened to create financial hardship that no one had told me about?

Momma saw my confusion and gave me my marching orders. "You want it bad enough, you need to find the money to buy it on your own."

Find the money? Did people *find* money? That was a bold concept. Taking her words literally, I began to search for loose change everywhere I went. You'd be surprised at how many quarters and other lesser denominations of change you can find if you go looking. Single dollar bills too. Once I found a $10 bill on the street. This seemed like a well-kept secret that I wasn't sure everyone should know about.

My mom, teaching me to be resourceful, didn't help me.

In fact, she seemed certain that I'd give up. Other relatives appeared to be more impressed by my hustle. The money started filling up this toy treasure chest that had been given to me earlier. But when I did my first accounting and saw that I had a ways to go, I got bolder. If I happened to be at my grandfather's house, say, and spotted some change up on his bureau, I'd ask if he wanted me to put it to good use. Call it early practice in selling others on investment—in me.

When the day came that I was able to count out the $50, I had to go immediately to Walmart to make the big purchase. Nobody even suggested that I might want to go to the bank first and get the coins changed into dollar bills. Nope. Hustle once again told me—*Now!* Momma drove us there, and I marched up to the electronics counter and presented the chest, opening it to show its contents, and then asked for the game that I wanted.

The salesman was impressed. "You collected all this yourself, $50?"

"I found it!"

He looked at me in amazement as if it had never occurred to him that people would ignore that much money lying around and it took an eight-year-old junior hustler to put his nose to the ground and scoop it all up.

My mother assured the man that I'd done it all on my own. The pride I felt in myself and the pride she took in my accomplishment were the two best feelings in the world, surpassed only at that time by the thrill of owning and playing that game.

Hustle. It's simple—if you can't afford the life you want, you'll have to find the money for yourself. The lesson would reverberate into my teens and young adult years as a reminder of the power of my own resourcefulness and the need to do the legwork required of all ambitious undertakings.

Since those days, I've learned that resourcefulness, hustle, and hood wisdom can be found in many communities. It's probably safe to assume that you have family members who have also made much of opportunities in their lives thanks to their own version of hustle.

Some of us are lucky enough to have an elder like my Big Ma in the family. My great-grandmother was born with a work ethic that could put a grown man to shame. She literally worked until the day she died. My Big Ma had an optimism you could see and feel from her, a belief that no matter how harsh the conditions, there were solutions to problems on the other side of the mountain—you just couldn't see them until you climbed those rocky cliffs. She had a deeply spiritual value system and her hood wisdom was almost psychic. If she had a bad feeling about a decision or a travel plan, that was it, no ifs, ands, or buts. She'd make a pronouncement and I would listen. The resource of a finely tuned intuition can be absolutely indispensable for an entrepreneur or executive.

The other example of hustle in the more conventional sense came from one of my aunts who climbed the ladder in retail management. She didn't have a college education but wore her love for her job on her sleeve, from the lowest rungs all the way up. My aunt was one of those people who dared to shine and to strive for excellence. She wasn't doing anything especially glamorous, but she saw the big picture and carried herself as if she were a CEO of a top corporation. Over time it paid off, rewarding her with job security, savings, and benefits for herself and her family. Her hustle was legit. Out of the whole family, she was the one member who stayed afloat when times were tough. Hers was the practicality that comes with hood wisdom, and I admired her for it.

Enthusiasm for what you do—even if it's just what's going to get you to that next place—is an underrated resource. In the hood, sometimes you're supposed to play it cool and not show enthusiasm—that is, unless it's going to reap you a load of cash right away. Being overly enthusiastic about school or work can get you labeled as corny or, as I knew well, a geek. That's where you can start to see the limitations to hood wisdom.

In the rest of the world, trying to restrain your focus

and passion is not a winning approach. One of the most important ingredients of a successful college application or scholarship award essay comes down to how contagiously you convey your enthusiasm. This applies equally to interviewing for jobs and pitching ideas for investments. Enthusiasm is actually an aspect of hustle but one that is too often underrated.

One other example of hustle that I observed growing up is hard to define, yet you know this unapologetic approach when you see it. It can be almost intangible as to how this straight-up hustle mentality works, and it's also nearly compulsive. One of my uncles, an incorrigible hustler, personified what I'm talking about. My uncle could sweet-talk and seduce any woman, married or not, into opening up her arms, her home, her checkbook, and you can name what all else, just to enjoy the pleasure of his company.

When I say "intangible" I mean, in this case, that nobody could figure out what exactly made my uncle so appealing. And by "compulsive" I mean he couldn't stop himself. He knew it wasn't quite right, but somehow the temptation was not easy to resist—around any woman he was like a bank robber walking past a bank with an open vault and nobody guarding it.

My uncle's major resource was a way with words and their ability to make every woman feel like she was the most important person in the world to him (in that moment) and even if he was unworthy (he was), he swore that without her he was nothing. He even put it out there that he was already involved with someone else. The women all seemed to respond by wanting to take care of him. His charm as a straight-up hustler was that it came with no apologies. He was totally authentic. What's crazy is that the more upfront he was about his limitations and lack of availability, the more desirable he became. Watching him work a room was a master class in hustle—not that I appreciated it at the time.

My uncle used sales hustle to let his customers sell themselves on him. That's not a strategy that always works, but it's an alternative to a hard sell. When you make your "customers" feel loved and appreciated while also letting them know you are not available, that is a tried-and-true sales technique that taps a resource known as *exclusivity*. We've all experienced wanting what we can't have. Many high-end brands operate on the appeal of exclusivity. Advertisers for years have competed to get the hottest celebrities from entertainment and sports to sign lavish endorsement deals. Having them associated with a brand gives it allure and desirability that a customer can only obtain by spending the money.

There were limits, I learned, to the hood appeal of unavailability. By the way, my uncle eventually did get his comeuppance when enough of the women he hustled got mad at him. Likewise, in the real world of marketing, you want more than brand desirability and exclusivity. I learned a lot about that with some of my early start-up ventures.

That being said, I give credit to anyone who is an unapologetic, straight-up hustler. I've seen it in the tech start-up space, where I've been wowed by creative presentations that grab your interest right away. You might not want to bank on them actually living up to their own hype, but going all-in on a pitch is a worthy marketing skill. Investors like to be wooed and made to think they're special, so the exclusivity lure can be a strong one. Once you get the money, though, the magic of hustle dissolves. Then you have to deliver.

A lot of the hood wisdom I learned up until the age of twelve or thirteen was absorbed unconsciously just watching examples of hustle around me. As a child, that's all I knew. But when I started to hear lecturers talking about subjects like financial literacy and entrepreneurship, it did start to occur to me that there were limits to street smarts and that hustle alone was not going to be enough to take me where I wanted to go.

At the same time, I've also come to the conclusion that in this vastly uncertain, changing, historic, and unpredictable period, your survival will depend on your resourcefulness—your grind combined with old-fashioned ingenuity.

Hustle and hood wisdom have relevance in the academic and scientific worlds, for innovators and founders of start-ups, and for investors. Hustle is needed for leaders and followers of social movements and for students of history.

When combined with other resources in my wheelhouse—like scholarship—hood wisdom was necessary for helping me find my edge. In the early stages of becoming a social entrepreneur, I gained confidence from that edge that maybe one day I could take on such antagonists as widespread, systemic racism and poverty.

Resourcefulness, as I've defined hustle, doesn't have to be part of your background or your biography. Sometimes you find that capacity because you don't have any other choice. You have to learn to develop and use what you already have. You may know this from your own experiences of facing a sudden challenge or taking on a difficult undertaking.

If not, or if you feel overwhelmed by uncertainty, my advice is to go looking for someone who is resourceful and can give you some pointers. During my childhood and teen years—when I continued to pray for the wisdom of Solomon and continued to keep my nose to the ground for resources others seemed to miss—I unapologetically sought out role models, mentors, and champions like Dr. Starks and others. I also will admit to something that's probably more common than most people are willing to acknowledge—some of my mentors weren't real or alive.

It's true. Before actual mentors came along, some of the heroes who served as my best role models for success came from the worlds of fiction and fantasy and from the pages of literature and history.

I've heard my peers complain that they didn't have any of those positive examples when they were growing up. Here's what I usually tell them: do your own authentic hustle and look for guidance that's there for you for the asking, often in the most surprising forms.

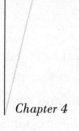

Chapter 4

How Grit Makes
Batman Fly

I have one power. I never give up.

—Batman/Bruce Wayne

There is one question that I hear most often when I'm on the lecture circuit, especially when speaking to students getting ready to apply for scholarships and for admission to college or grad school. They invariably ask: *What is it that the scholarship and admission people are most looking for?*

There are a few answers to that question, as I learned from my own experience and from asking it of countless decision makers. But the one answer that I hear consistently from experts is that you need to be able *to tell your story.*

Scholarship review panels, like college admissions reviewers, want a story that lets them feel like they've met you and have been on your journey. They want to know what sets you apart and makes you different, who and what inspires and motivates you, what influences and role models have shaped you, how you've applied wisdom you've learned through adversity, and developed strength, resilience, and humor. Again, they are looking for evidence of ways that you've demonstrated initiative and been part of something bigger than yourself. They want to feel that you'll be an asset for their campus, alumni foundation, or organization down the road, maybe even the face on a victory poster for their legacy—so they can claim a role in your success. They want a story that has you jumping off the page, often in five hundred words or less. They want a story that makes them feel like you're sitting in the room with them.

Another answer that I hear a lot from folks who review these essays is that they are looking to see if an applicant has *grit*. In recent years, the word "grit" has become somewhat overused. That's why, experts say, you want to *show* rather than *tell* the reviewers that you have it. Kind of like hustle, having grit conjures a range of connotations and meanings. Psychologists view grit as a positive personality trait that reveals a person's tenacity in pursuit of a goal. University of Pennsylvania professor Angela Lee Duckworth—who literally wrote the book on grit—defines it as living life "as a marathon not a sprint" and calls it a special blend of passion and perseverance. Grit is also associated with traits such as fortitude—having courage even in the face of fear, remaining determined even after failure or loss, and generally showing strength of character.

One international grad school program in psychology reported that educators at every level agreed that IQ was only one factor separating their best and worst students. Just as important to their students' success was grit. In fact, teachers and psychologists have come to a consensus in recent years that grit may well be the leading predictor of success—personally, academically, and professionally. The aspects of grit most emphasized by these authorities are courage, conscientiousness, perseverance against all odds, independence, purpose, and, again, passion.

All of this is helpful to know, I realize, but when it comes to telling only one or two stories from your life that reveal who you are and that you hope will show your grit, these generalities may complicate matters for you. My solution—and I can definitely recommend you give it a try—is to look at your heroes, your mentors, champions, and role models, real or imaginary, and check out how grit informed their story.

You may be surprised by how much you learn about yourself when you look at the examples of success in others that you embraced in your formative years. This will help you identify your own story of grit, whether you're applying to college or for a scholarship, looking for a job or a promotion, marketing your business or mounting a political campaign. Ask yourself, as I did: *How did you first learn grit?*

Each of us is born into circumstances not of our choosing. We are handed a story—a set of circumstances, characters, and plot points—that creates a starting narrative for our lives. For many individuals, that narrative can be allowed to define you and sweep you up into its own trajectory. For others, that's the story that shapes but doesn't ultimately determine your eventual path. Then there are still others whose stories include generations of poverty, teenage pregnancy, lack of education, oppression, bigotry, family dysfunction, and worse. We're rarely surprised when their stories going forward continue to carry those elements. What is surprising is when you see someone who decides to rewrite history and tell an entirely different story from the narrative that was inherited.

My belief is that *we do have a choice as to whether we accept or reject the limitations put in front of us*. We can choose instead to tell ourselves the story we want to be ours.

In other words, you get to determine who you become either *because* of the story you were handed or *in spite of it*. Here's the hitch: even when you decide not to be defined by your circumstances, how can you become something you can't see in front of you?

My answer goes to the same process I used in seeking wisdom. You always have the option to look for heroes and role models everywhere you can—including in the example of individuals who may not be known to you personally. In my case, I have long been drawn to the stories of people who, in spite of their tough beginnings, used their hidden advantages and gifts in inspiring ways.

From as far back as I can remember, I adopted famous and lesser-known figures from history, fiction, entertainment, business—you name it—not just as role models but almost as members of my family! They were heroic in a lot of ways yet also flawed. The appeal of the heroes I chose, though I didn't know it at the time, was that they seemed to embody grit. Somehow their stories resonated with mine.

Early on, yes, there were the video-game characters I admired. All of them were gritty underdogs, so much so that the David versus Goliath theme, by itself, became part of my narrative. In video games like *Final Fantasy* and *Kingdom Hearts*, winning always came down to using hidden assets to gain knowledge. One of the characters pointed out, "One who knows nothing can understand nothing." If winning every math, spelling, or history contest meant not fitting in and being cast as a nerd, so be it. If I could tell myself that being ridiculed was temporary and I would come out on top, with knowledge as my sword, I felt more powerful.

When it came to superheroes in comics and on the big

screen, I honestly loved all of them—from the mutants of Marvel's *X-Men* to DC Comics' *Superman*. My favorite, though, hands down, as I touched on earlier, was Batman, who I met not at the movies or in a comic book but on TV.

That old 1960s live-action TV series starring Adam West as Batman/Bruce Wayne was pivotal for me. Network daytime television reran it in the 1990s when I was around seven or eight years old. In my memory, I can see myself that first time I witnessed the series. It seemed to show up by magic on the TV. Over at my Big Ma's house, I was spread out on her old-fashioned rug in her den, just watching television one afternoon. With no advance warning, the show started and I heard that iconic musical theme. *Dadadadadadadada. . . . Batman!* It brought me up to my knees. The Batmobile was better than any cartoon superhero car. And the dialogue, to my ears at the time, sounded real and believable. What grabbed me was not so much what happened once Bruce Wayne put on his mask and cape and headed out to save Gotham but his story of being an orphan turned entrepreneur.

The name Bruce Wayne Enterprises jolted something inside me. There was something cool about being a businessman, even if I had no idea what "enterprises" meant. When I devoured everything I could from DC Comics, I learned that Bruce Wayne was born without special powers but because of his circumstances had chosen to create a superhero training regimen for himself. The story about how Bruce witnessed the murder of his parents got to me. He could have been destroyed by it; instead, he had to overcome his fear of being killed too by using everyday things around himself, including technology, to fully develop his mental and physical capacities. Those strengths, used strategically, empowered Batman to battle his foes and achieve justice for other victims. The idea was planted in me that somehow I too needed to master both business and technology.

It was Bruce Wayne who first exposed me to certain lessons about financial literacy that I had a chance to study more closely as an adolescent—starting with the critical revelation (to me) that it takes money to make money. Bruce used the earnings from his inherited family business to invest in the development of all his tech gadgets. Those in turn could be monetized to yield even more revenues. Of course, as a social entrepreneur (before that term existed), Bruce's earned wealth funded his philanthropy—which in turn gave him stature and influence.

Long before I thought that achieving enough financial power to make a difference for others was something maybe I could do one day, I saw in the example of a comic-book character that *it was possible.*

And anything is possible once you have imagined it. How did Bruce Wayne, mere mortal, become a superhero?

Like the quote says, by using one power—never giving up, aka grit. That spoke loudly to me.

We might not think of grit per se when we break down the seemingly superhuman things that Batman can do. Start with his ability to fly. You could argue that he is actually gliding, and that would be correct. But think of the trial and error, perseverance, and attention to detail required to design his bat-suit—complete with a cape that can become wings and boots that can give him spring. Think of the countless hours spent in mastering an understanding of wind vectors and learning the science necessary to catch the right air currents so he could perfect his takeoffs and landings.

Grit is not magic, but it is what makes Batman fly—even in the face of fear.

Bruce Wayne/Batman and his grit exposed me to the need sometimes to play the long game. As the greatest of all superhero detectives, he always took the time necessary to solve a mystery before jumping to conclusions. He had learned to do that when, in his early days, he sought out the most famous of all detectives in the world and went to study with him.

As an entrepreneur by day and a crime-fighter by night, Bruce recognizes that he has to abide by a moral compass that includes a set of ruling principles for his narrative—one that clearly goes where the path does not go. For one thing, Batman doesn't kill his enemies. For another, he believes in being of service and fighting for a cause larger than himself. He famously stands up to bullies, although he is flawed too: sometimes dark and brooding, Bruce is known for losing his temper. At the same time, he is an outspoken advocate for criminal rehabilitation because he believes that people are basically good.

That was probably the one Bruce Wayne stance I questioned. My feeling, as a realist, was that people are who they are and you can't ever really change individuals who don't want to be changed—especially the ones who perpetuate systemic racism and villainous injustice. Over in the Marvel universe where the heroic X-Men (and women) were marginalized as mutants, there was a parallel debate about human nature between Professor Xavier and Magneto. Serious fans have long inferred that Professor Xavier was inspired by the more idealistic view of human nature as represented by Dr. Martin Luther King Jr. (who strove to gain power through peaceful civil disobedience) while Magneto, said to represent Malcolm X, advocated the approach of achieving goals by any means necessary. Stan Lee would later deny that this message was intentional, but there are too many parallels in *Batman* to the different facets of the civil rights movement to be denied.

My feeling as a thirteen-year-old was that while I valued the ideals of Professor Xavier, in reality, when you are up against entrenched power, there is no negotiating. After all, when David went out to face Goliath, there was no negotiating.

Once I ventured off Shipwreck Island where I first discovered the need for grit, much to my surprise it turned out that I was not alone in seeking a form of empowerment from superhero stories. This was definitely true in the tech start-up arena. Then again, I'd been much more fully immersed in the worlds of my superheroes than many—to the point that I took a lead from Bruce Wayne and trained in martial arts during middle school.

Batman remained my favorite superhero from childhood on, most of all because he is considered a genius and the smartest of any in the DC Comics universe; his closest Marvel equivalent, Iron Man (Tony Stark), is also a genius, but there are others in the Marvel hierarchy smarter than Iron Man.

The tragedy Bruce Wayne experienced was different from mine, and he had access to money that I did not. But his grit was something I could muster, and he gave me courage. Applying the useful mantra of WWBWD ("What Would Bruce Wayne Do?"), I came to the conclusion that *those of us who have less have to learn to do more.* This was the long game I chose to play to pull myself out of poverty. If it made me a geek to follow a superhero, so be it.

All I could see around me in Birmingham, Alabama, were people giving up on their meaningful possibilities—

drug dealers, gangs, adults overdosing, kids left alone, families going without, everybody losing jobs, a community barely making ends meet. On the pages of DC Comics, I found a future that might have been fantasy, but it sustained me.

Maybe this can explain how ready I was to be mentored after my act of initiative—calling around for local resources—had led me to contact Dr. Karen Starks. Here is where the actual universe for regular human beings like you and me can be so powerful. Just as I was looking for a mentor like her, Dr. Starks was looking for a protégé like me.

Let me pause to underscore the message that Chance the Rapper and Jesse Williams would make so clear at an event for Chicago high school students that I hosted sometime later: when you pursue a path forward, no matter what your zip code, there are mentors and guides ready to cheer you on. It's up to you to go in search of them and to value how they can help.

This is especially true when you are in high school or college, or when you're getting ready to enter the working world. What's more, at a time of economic uncertainty, when many are being forced to reboot their career or reinvent their professional aspirations, there are organizations and individuals offering resources and guidance to people of all ages and in all situations.

Having grit and seeking your own route to success does not require you to do it *all* on your own. When you do go off the beaten path, you still may need to ask for directions now and then.

I became an entrepreneur at the age of fourteen, not because Dr. Starks necessarily taught me how to become one, but because she gave me the context in which to become one.

I'll never forget the evening Momma drove me to my first Community Entrepreneurship Institute meeting at the Innovation Depot in downtown Birmingham.

Momma, pleased that I'd found out about this eight-week program, looked at the impressive white building and asked again, "You gonna learn how to run a business here?"

I shrugged and nodded. "That's what they said. It's part of it."

She wished me good luck, and I hurried into the building. The office was empty, meaning I was that early, that excited. This was one of those inflection points when I felt the universe giving me a small tap on my shoulder—like this was where I was supposed to be.

Soon, before the other teens arrived, I met Dr. Karen Starks for the first time. She lit up the room and made me feel at home. Our connection was instantaneous, as if we'd already been having a conversation that had only been on pause.

I'd never met anyone with a doctorate before. Dr. Starks was not just brilliant, not just hyper-educated, but also super-positive, curious, analytical, and insightful. She was that first real-life role model who also looked after me as a kind of a parental figure.

Soon the other kids trickled in. We sat around a conference table, and Dr. Starks supplied snacks (basically dinner for most of us). There were about nine teenagers altogether, and only a handful of us really had any genuine interest in learning about how businesses are built. A few had been coerced into attending, maybe by a parent or guidance counselor, while some others had behavioral problems and probably were there just to give somebody else a break. One of them was a huge ghetto kid with violent tendencies—as I could personally attest after he tried to attack me. Dr. Starks resolved that situation quickly. Two of the girls were pregnant (or would soon be), and a couple of the others came from physically abusive backgrounds.

By this point in time I'd started to attend Ramsay High School, the magnet school that you had to test into, and many of my new friends were much like me: college-bound, academically motivated, and involved in a range of extra-curricular activities. Yet there was no class or after-school opportunity at Ramsay that taught entrepreneurship. Instead, I had to travel outside of my regular rounds.

That in itself was a lesson. When you follow the adage

"seek and ye shall find," or WWBWD, to solve a question, you may have to look for a while as you turn over all the stones. Grit will keep your nose to the ground until you've found what you're looking for.

Dr. Starks was of the belief that by exposing young people to knowledge they'd never seen at home or in their neighborhoods, you could help set them on a better track to success. Sometimes she was right and sometimes, again, as I'd concluded, it was hard to change mindsets that had been conditioned over several years. If you want to change minds, I believe, the key is to find a mind that is at least hungry for something different from the familiar. Needless to say, I was in that category, along with a couple of the other kids. Despite our environments, we were wired to want something other than what we knew.

One of our first projects was to start a mock business with the purpose of producing events and entertainment for tweens and teens in Birmingham. Channeling my inner Bruce Wayne, I made a pitch for why I was the obvious choice for CEO. I won unanimously by voice vote—after running unopposed, of course. Our mission was to create safe and fun entertainment for middle school and high school youth that gave kids somewhere to go after school and on weekends. Our focus was to be strategic by trying it just once as a test run.

Dr. Starks laid out the steps. We wrote a mission statement, established our goals and values, and named our enterprise: Tweens and Teens Entertainment, Inc. We also elected a board of directors and other executives and prepared a business plan for our first live event, which involved producing a day of activities, games, and informative demonstrations, complete with decorations, food, and old-fashioned fun for Birmingham's teenage citizens. I oversaw the selection of a venue in a donated church hall and conceived the main attraction of an obstacle course that would become the talk of the event. In the hopes of encouraging the county to tout the possibilities, we managed to coordinate with the Jefferson County Health Department and established a follow-up forum with community leaders. We also had to figure out how we could get donations from local businesses to avoid having to charge admission. As the project had been given seed money in the form of a grant, we also had to create a budget and then look for how to coordinate with businesses and nonprofits to help cosponsor the event for youth.

This was the first time that I had experienced the metamorphosis that happens when you take an idea that exists only in your head or on paper and then turn it into a reality. On the eve of the day we planned to go live with the first Tweens and Teens Entertainment, Inc., event, I asked Dr. Starks, "Can you give me any advice for how I could improve as CEO?"

She said frankly, "No, you are a natural leader. Trust that." No one had ever verbalized that to me. She asked if anyone in my family was going to attend or help out. Embarrassed, I replied that they wanted to come but had obligations. The truth was that they couldn't understand why I'd choose to spend extra time doing something like this. Dr. Starks needed no further explanation. She understood that my mother was young—still in her twenties—and that she and the rest of the family had a hard time relating to my interests. Dr. Starks said something kind anyway, along the lines of "Well, I'm sure they must be proud of you." And we left it at that.

Part of being a leader and having grit, I realized then, was about not necessarily being given the applause or credit you have coming. None of that mattered—especially not when I saw the faces of the kids who showed up for our event. They looked like they had arrived at Disneyland (something I wouldn't experience for years to come). Rainbow-colored lights flashed from different angles, food stands offered pizza and cheese-covered nachos, and there was a dance floor that we'd managed to emblazon temporarily with our logo.

In Bruce Wayne style, and at very little expense, I had headed up an ambitious undertaking, I had motivated my team, and we had built an attraction for the youth of my city. We packed the hall.

I felt like Batman without the mask or cape. We made a little profit from refreshments, but on top of that I felt the rush of being a person of influence, not to mention that we had done some good. The laughter of the teens and tweens was something that I'd never forget. No one had ever tried anything like it, and we pulled it off. Years later, as an entrepreneur, I'd find myself creating similar events aimed at promoting ways of making college more affordable, and I'd feel the same.

Once you know you can turn your limitation into opportunity, once you do it that first time, you know you can most likely do it again on a larger scale. It was how I imagined flying to be for Batman. You get past your fears, glide just a little off the ground, and can't wait until you try it again.

So that's what I did. The next effort was a solo flight that came about because I had to find a solution to a problem—one that directly affected me.

Toward the beginning of my junior year of high school, notoriously the most demanding for any high-performing college-bound student, I started to seriously research everything needed for college admissions. This was, incidentally, at the height of the economic collapse of 2008, and I was already beginning to stress about having a roof over our heads or not enough to eat. Even before I could think about how to pay for college, it hit me one day that other than my involvement with Tweens and Teens Entertainment, Inc. I had few volunteer hours on my high school résumé.

This was a problem, as I knew that the most competitive colleges would look closely at hours spent outside of those required by academic studies and the usual school extracurricular activities. Ironically, in our inner-city neighborhoods where there was so much need, there were almost no charities or causes offering volunteer hours. Weirdly, all the opportunities to volunteer were offered in suburban, more affluent communities.

My Call to Action was an idea that came to me to connect local student volunteers like me to national and local charitable organizations that needed to have us on their radar. My brainstorm was for a nonprofit that I founded and called Genesis. My first step was to form alliances with such organizations as the American Cancer Society and its Relay for Life annual fundraiser, Habitat for Humanity, and Birmingham's Jimmie Hale Mission, which targets such issues as homelessness, addiction, and "poverty thinking." My plan was to start with better-known charities and then add local partners.

At first, nobody returned my phone calls. Not one to give up, I kept trying until finally I decided to make a personal appearance at the offices of the Jimmie Hale Mission— where I was referred to a volunteer coordinator who was in desperate need. Another lesson learned. There is little that can compete with a personal contact. You know what else? As soon as we had one organization interested in student volunteers, the others were happy to say yes.

My next step was to sign up a major percentage of fellow students from Ramsay High School. As the year progressed, students from other Birmingham high schools reached out to Genesis to get on our volunteer list. Genesis—named, of course, for the first book of the Old Testament—took off and became a force for good in the community.

What had begun as a personal concern about not having enough volunteer hours for my college applications had turned into not just a personal solution for me and my fellow volunteers, but a minor paradigm shift on a local level. Ambitiously, I created a slogan for Genesis: "We are the beginning of the future and the origin of success."

Aside from volunteer opportunities involving puppies (I love them), the most moving experience I had was heading up a group of students to perform at Jessie's Place, a residential program for women that was part of the Jimmie Hale Mission. We sang, played instruments, read poetry, and read inspirational writing. One of my good friends who was on my team told me that a relative of hers was a resident. Seeing the two connect in person was a profoundly moving experience. We were all in tears.

Forming Genesis—a major success that would last until some years after I graduated—had proven to be another pivotal experience. Whenever I told people about the concept and the scope of our efforts to match volunteers with good causes, they'd scratch their heads and ask me (or themselves): *Huh, why'd nobody else ever think of that?*

Some would scoff and admit it was a great idea, but

wasn't I in over my head? Nope, I'd tell them, and then I'd go to work like a dog to prove them wrong for even suggesting there was such a thing as thinking too big. Genesis helped my college applications and those of a whole lot of other students too. We showed our collective grit on a schoolwide basis, and we helped leading charities. We learned what service is all about.

Let me assure you that if you have been known to have an idea that strikes others as so obvious they should have thought of it, or that makes them react jealously to the point of suggesting somebody more capable should be given the idea, just smile and pat yourself on the back. You are on your way.

You are becoming an entrepreneur, asking yourself WWBWD, and then, with hustle and grit, taking the next steps toward bringing your idea to life. I'll repeat—you never have to get permission to think like a superhero, especially the superheroes who are actually human like you.

That said, I want to return to the topic raised earlier about how to best tell your authentic story—or that of your enterprise. Without question, that was the major challenge in front of me when it came to applying for outside scholarships and college admissions, and later when promoting my business. This isn't a challenge that comes along just once. In my view, the ability to communicate your story to others, to achieve buy-in, is important at every stage of the game.

What helps immensely—and I can only recommend you give it a shot—is to add to that inventory you may have already started (the one that includes your goals and values) by jotting down some of the lessons, people, achievements, and failures that shaped you. Look again at the traits we discussed that are associated with grit. When did you first experience what it is to spread your wings and fly? Your own authentic, original story is there in the fine print of your life to date, just waiting to be expanded and told.

Chapter 5

There Are No Wrong Turns When You Go Where There Is No Path

Only those who risk going too far can possibly find out how far one can go.

—T. S. Eliot

Whenever I hear people talk about their formative years, I realize that the reference point may be different for many of us. Generally, however, we are talking about the experiences that formed us as individuals and that formed a bridge between our childhood and adulthood. Some have pinpointed that transition as usually occurring between the ages of eleven and nineteen. That's not necessarily a rule, though, because some of us had to grow up really young, for many reasons, while some of us don't get a chance to move into adulthood completely until later in life.

WHERE and WHEN your formative years happened is relevant for a few reasons when it comes to understanding and telling your story. These markers don't have to define who you are, but they create the backdrop for the experiences that led to your own discoveries of who you are.

Those life-changing, self-defining moments of discovery may happen in good times or bad, in familiar or foreign places, when you have been chasing after a goal or when you aren't even expecting something important to take place. What is so powerful—even magical—about these experiences is that they give you a kind of map that can guide you to your future.

This map is not a technical, tried-and-true GPS for how you are supposed to navigate every turn. It's more like a signaling system that reminds you of your priorities and the awesome journey you've chosen to follow without a set path in front of you. It's an article of faith, forged by those experiences, that lets you navigate through all kinds of uncertainty and turbulence. Your faith in your higher power and in yourself is a reminder that there are never going to be any wrong turns if you are willing to go where the path doesn't lead.

You will make mistakes, you'll fail, you'll take a wrong turn, and you'll feel fear. Yet your faith will keep you going. The lessons learned from your self-defining moments can be hard-won. If you choose to take them to heart and put them to use in writing your own success story, they will become your greatest assets.

Those experiences were not only the ones that I described as self-defining in my admissions and scholarship essays, they also came in useful when I entered the business world. When I was first going out to get investments in my start-ups, my ability to tap early lessons helped my vision to expand and grow. My formative years taught me how to have transformative power—how to turn misfortune into knowledge and poverty into gold.

Your experiences, whenever and wherever they take place, can give you the same transformative power. If that sounds like too big of a leap for you to contemplate in a time of uncertainty, maybe my story will convince you otherwise.

When I think back to my formative high school years, the immortal opening of *A Tale of Two Cities* by Charles Dickens comes to mind:

> It was the best of times, it was the worst of times, it was the age of wisdom, it was the age of foolishness, it was the epoch of belief, it was the epoch of incredulity, it was the season of Light, it was the season of Darkness, it was the spring of hope, it was the winter of despair,

we had everything before us, we had nothing before us, we were all going direct to Heaven, we were all going direct the other way—in short, the period was so far like the present period, that some of its noisiest authorities insisted on its being received, for good or for evil, in the superlative degree of comparison only.

When I first read those words at eighteen years old, they helped me see that the best of times of my high school years so far would help give me the resilience and faith to get through the worst of times of that era. Unmanageable conditions, both personal and widespread, had been peaking in my home life and all around me, and the economic pressure cooker was taking a tough toll on Birmingham and devastating the Black community.

Let me start on the negative side of the ledger. In 2006 there were only early tremors of the coming financial meltdown caused primarily by toxic financial instruments called derivatives (which everyone knew were a recipe for disaster) and the subprime mortgage lending collapse. Most places in the country hadn't yet started to feel those tremors that would lead to the Great Recession, but we had in Birmingham. A shortage in affordable housing was already hitting hard by the time the banks and lending institutions started to falter and the job market dried up. By 2007, Momma had her hands full with a new baby, the first of my two younger siblings, and the other one was on the way. She no longer had a second job (and no one could afford her bookkeeping services), but she had held on to a job answering phones at a call center for a good while. Then she was let go and the call center went overseas.

To this day, I know that my mother never saw us as experiencing homelessness, but the truth is, we did not have a place of our own for extended periods. That had to be terrible for her as a single mom of three, especially with those three being a toddler, a baby, and a teenager. Thankfully, we could stay with various family members until Momma got back on her feet. Yet the logistics were still awkward because where we could stay would change periodically. My stress was amplified by trying to figure out how to help however I could financially, even if it was just by not having to be fed, and how to stay focused on my plan to "get off the island" by going away to college.

Every day was like a sprint and a marathon both. There was school, homework, AP test prep classes, other college entrance exam tests (SATs, ACTs) and meetings, volunteer hours, and my activities running Genesis. In my junior year, I began my college admissions research, which involved staying after school at its library and making trips to the public library as well. My mother made it clear that I couldn't just show up at night when it was time to sleep, even though I was dependent on others for rides and that made getting in at a certain time difficult.

On a few occasions, I mouthed off at her. Not my

proudest moments. The last time I did so, muttering something sarcastic under my breath, she calmly and quietly grabbed my smartphone from me and told me she'd give it back when she was good and ready.

Of course, I knew where she would hide it and how to get it back. My real concern was that she was willing to jeopardize my ability to find out where to go for my AP study group, or to get a text from whoever was supposed to show up to volunteer at the Ronald McDonald House event. Praying for some wisdom, I was able to see her lack of control over our situation—and that she did love me and wanted the best for me. My solution was to go stay with my grandfather—who lived downtown and close to Ramsay High School. Momma must have been relieved, because when I did manage to swipe my phone back, she only shrugged and said, "What took you so long to find it?"

The arrangement was that I'd stay with my grandfather during the week and go to be with Momma and my baby siblings on the weekends. There were some days in between, though, when I wasn't sure where I was going to sleep that night.

At the time, I can assure you that I felt the constant weight of shame—embarrassment—that we had fallen through the cracks. We weren't alone, by the way. In fact, during the worst of the economic tribulations of the Great Recession, Alabama was harder hit with job loss than any other southern state. Birmingham and Hoover, one of its suburbs, saw the most jobs lost across the state. The national recovery of 2009 would pick up steam within the year, but it would not be until 2011 that the Magic City got some of its mojo back.

Meanwhile, a feeling of powerlessness had begun to set in. Not only over my situation but even more so out of concern for my family and a whole lot of folks around us. Crime rose. Drugs and gang activity increased, as did the number of high school dropouts and teen pregnancies. Charities serving poor and marginalized communities couldn't accommodate the sheer need, and many lost funding when sponsors couldn't afford to help.

As usual, I tried to tune out the negativity, but I can remember in the spring of my junior year starting to question myself. Teachers and my guidance counselor had suggested that I consider staying local for college. Relatives questioned me about even needing to get a secondary education.

One night after explaining to my grandfather that his old computer was unable to connect to the internet, I tried to hurry out, adding, "I gotta go to the library to get online and check out a college. "

"What college?"

When I answered him that it happened to be the University of Pennsylvania in Philadelphia, my grandfather more or less said I was fooling myself. He peppered me with questions. How much did it cost to go there? How much did it cost even to apply? Why Philadelphia? Why not the University of Alabama? Why even go to college? Why wait another five years before I could earn a real living?

I told him about the Wharton School of business, one of the most prestigious business schools in the nation, housed at Penn. He waved his hand like, *Wharton? Who you tryin' to impress?* Like, *Dream on, Chris.*

He wasn't trying to be mean. But that was a NO that hit a nerve. What if I wasn't good enough? What if hustle, grit, and scholarship weren't enough? What if, despite great grades and test scores and volunteer hours and strong recommendations, I wasn't deserving enough to go? I'd heard that athletes could get full-ride scholarships at top schools—some of them called it getting their "scholly"— but I wasn't an athlete. If life were fair, nobody would have to be poor, and nobody would have to lose sleep over getting a decent education or not. If life were fair, nobody would have to endure feeling that access to opportunity exists only for those who already have opportunity.

But life isn't always fair. The thought of not being good enough for the best universities to welcome me was too much to bear. Worse, honestly, was the notion that poverty was a stain that could never be removed. Like a Catch-22. If education was the great springboard to opportunity and wealth, but an education was out of reach for all but the well-to-do, the connected, and a lucky gifted few, that was economic injustice pure and simple—and a recipe for a spiral of escalating social problems. There had to be a better way. It was too soul-crushing to think that I was supposed to give up everything I'd believed could be possible.

I rushed out of my grandfather's house fighting tears. The ground felt like it was sinking under my feet.

My friend who was giving me a ride to the library had to make sure I was okay. I told her it was nothing, even though I was still on the verge of breaking down.

As soon as I got on a computer at the library and began my virtual tour of Penn, I felt my spirits lift. There was something inviting about Philadelphia that called to me— the City of Brotherly Love, the history, Benjamin Franklin, the Liberty Bell, and all the architectural landmarks. Out of curiosity, I started looking at websites for other universities in the Philly area—Temple, Drexel, Villanova, and others. They all had a lot to offer. Penn had the Wharton School, the oldest business school in the world, a beautiful campus, and classrooms in iconic buildings that looked like scenes from Hogwarts in *Harry Potter*. At the same time, I was drawn to aspects of other universities, and I was especially impressed by Drexel—even to the point of feeling one of those little taps from the universe making sure I was paying attention to this one.

Drexel also had a prestigious business school, LeBow, and something for all undergrads that I hadn't seen offered anywhere else—an entrepreneurship degree. Both Penn and Drexel at the time cost over $50,000 a year for tuition, room, and board. That didn't include books and supplies, travel, clothes, toiletries, medicine, or food and lodging during holidays. (And both of the two universities' costs would go up to over $60,000 a year by the time I graduated.)

The reality check almost knocked me out of my chair. More than $200,000 to attend a four-year program? Obviously, I could apply for financial aid—which was need-based—and that was encouraging, but that didn't mean I was guaranteed a full-ride "scholly." Drexel intrigued me because of the option to do a five-year program with a semester's worth of a co-op that let you get real-world experience working in your field of interest and earning up to $15,000. Plus, I liked Drexel's emphasis on innovation and nontraditional pathways to success.

This was the first instance I can recall when, in the midst of the "it was the worst of times" crisis of my formative years, I put the images of specific universities and specific campuses next to my lofty but generic goal of going away to a northeastern college. Penn and Drexel were both right up there in my mind. Seeing myself inhabiting that world felt good and powerful and filled me with hope. Dr. Starks had been right to tell me to explore these campuses and their environs online.

In a matter of a few hours, I'd rewired my brain, going

from a state of despair to being fired up with motivation—from feeling trapped and at a dead end to beginning a transformational journey.

This is what I mean about a self-defining moment. The lesson, big and bold, got through to me. Uncertainty-induced fear has a remedy—information.

Now all I had to do was come up with $200,000 between financial aid and outside scholarships.

That realization caused me to almost laugh out loud. Twenty dollars was a lot of money to me at that time. My grandfather's voice still echoed. Who was I fooling? *Maybe*, I thought, *I should lower my sights.*

Hell, no.

And that was when the advice given to me a couple of years earlier came back loud and clear—to start looking and applying for as many outside scholarship awards as possible before applying to college. Could I do that? It was March 2009. I had seven and a half months to go before all my focus had to be on admissions applications.

Hell, yeah!

Seven and a half months to basically do what I had done, nose to the ground and with grit and hustle, as an eight-year-old trying to find overlooked money, though now the process was not unlike trying to find a needle in a haystack.

Could I do it? Well, honestly, I had no idea. All I could do was try. I could do a Bruce Wayne training regimen and become the greatest scholarship detective in the world.

Every spare minute could be devoted to this task and making this enormous wager, as there was no promise it would yield any success at all. How would I know, though, if I didn't give it my all?

None of my reclaimed self-belief was a guarantee that I'd get even one scholarship award. That same night, trying to go to sleep and starting to do my research on my rustic smartphone, I couldn't help being daunted by the odds of winning some of the most sought-after scholarships—most in the range of the Coca-Cola Foundation's onetime $20,000 award but going all the way to probably the most coveted one: the Gates Millennium Scholarship from the Bill and Melinda Gates Foundation for financially needy minority students who qualified as US citizens. Applicants had to be in good academic standing and be able to demonstrate the following:

- An outstanding academic record in high school (in the top 10 percent of his or her graduating class)

- Leadership ability (for example, as shown through participation in community service, extracurricular activities, or other activities)

- Exceptional personal success skills (such as emotional maturity, motivation, perseverance, and so on)

Selected scholars would receive funding for the full cost of attendance (tuition, fees, room, board, books, transportation, and even personal costs) not already covered by other financial aid. The Millennium Scholarship would be given annually for the duration of a scholar's higher education—including an undergraduate degree, master's, and doctorate.

In sum, the Millennium Scholarship was valued at more than $1 million.

The internal echo of NOs scoffed at my odds. We were going through the Great Recession, and there had to be thousands upon thousands of financially needy high school applicants with stellar academic records. My grades were excellent, true, but I had one subject coming up that worried me—calculus. In my senior year I would have to take AP Calculus, and the class had the makings of being my downfall.

The YES I used to counter that fear was the hope that my story would allow me to stand out. Those award amounts danced in my imagination.

A part of me wanted desperately to believe that I would qualify for the most competitive scholarships. Another part thought it would be wonderful to win any one of the smaller awards—for $500, $1,000, or $2,500. And then I realized what I'd forgotten, what my Big Ma always told me—have *faith*. When you can't make it one way, you find another way.

It was going to work out, however it was supposed to happen: whether I left town or stayed in Alabama, whether I went to the biggest marquee named university or a lesser-known school but with marvelous educators. My higher power asked me to have faith, and so I did—without neglecting to do the work required.

Faith is not easy to have when you are living in what seems to you to be the worst of times. When those times happen in your formative years and you are able to muster the will to see the possibilities for yourself and accept that you are on a path that is leading you somewhere great, faith becomes a fuel unlike any other. Faith can be self-defining and formative, letting you know that the rest of your life can be golden.

You don't have to believe in a higher power to have faith. It's a state of oneness with the present, an acceptance that you are its student and that if you look for the hidden good, you'll find it.

The hidden good for me—the best of times—wasn't so hidden.

To backtrack briefly and recall what was on the plus side of the ledger of my formative years, I will say that from the moment I arrived at Ramsay High School at the start of ninth grade, I felt the same sense of belonging that had been there instantly when I joined the teen empowerment group headed up by Dr. Starks.

I have a vivid recollection of when I walked into a classroom at Ramsay for the first period of the first day of ninth grade and the first person I met almost instantaneously became my best friend. Where I was an extrovert, in constant motion, in charge, talkative, and, yes, short, DeShaun, a star basketball player, was laid-back, laconic, introspective, and six-foot-four. We were a sight, I'm sure, walking down the hall, but we cracked each other up even more. DeShaun was fortunate to come from a middle-class family—his dad was a pastor and his mom a teacher—yet he and I were like-minded in many respects, with the same kinds of goals and values. Though I never met his family or visited their home, I could see how lucky he was to have that solid foundation, and vicariously I learned from it. His upbringing had set him on a more prescribed path than mine, though a successful one that would later include marriage and the pursuit of a career as a dentist. We are great friends to this day.

We were part of an extended family of friends too. We had true school spirit.

Located along the southern edge of downtown on a hilltop overlooking the city to the north, Ramsay also had views to the south of the peaks of what was called the Mountain of Iron. The entire enrollment—freshman through senior classes—was a little over seven hundred students, almost like a private school. Like DeShaun, most of my classmates were motivated and college-bound. To my knowledge, though, there weren't many as focused as I was on going out of state to college.

At Ramsay, one of my favorite places to be on campus was in the library—whether I was studying, doing my scholarship and college research, writing essays, or, after hours, getting a chance just to run ideas by our exceptional librarian, Deborah Stoves Holloway. She became a vital source of reassurance that I'd find the right college and find the money to be able to afford to go away. Ms. Holloway, who began her teaching career as a science teacher, had gone where the path didn't lead after first receiving her BS degree in biology/zoology and a master's in biology education from Alabama A&M University, before taking an unexpected turn toward earning advanced degrees in library sciences from the University of Alabama at Birmingham, as well as certification in library education media from Alabama State University.

As a library media specialist at Ramsay, Ms. Holloway was a computer and technology wiz, a proud African-American scholar of Black history, and a woman who had that enterprising, upbeat personality of someone always striving to uplift students—just as she uplifted herself. Whenever we talked about my process of looking for scholarships and archiving them for future use, Ms. Holloway would encourage and validate my efforts.

When she asked why I wanted to keep track of the scholarships with criteria that weren't a fit for me, I told her, "I might meet someone who could use that information down the road." She smiled as if to say, *Why hasn't anyone else thought of that before?* We talked about lack of access and affordability for most everyone besides the wealthiest students, not to mention the problem of rising student debt. That's when I confided that my goal was to win as much outside scholarship money as possible to supplement whatever financial aid I could get.

When I told her about the hundreds of thousands of dollars (later I'd learn that it's millions) going unclaimed, Ms. Holloway reacted much as Dr. Starks had—with disbelief. Such a well-kept secret of that proportion seemed like something somebody would have uncovered before. For the moment I decided to keep it quiet, until I had a chance to apply for as many award submissions as I could handle, using the system I'd developed.

As a scientist of biology/zoology turned library and media educator, Ms. Holloway encouraged my approach to systemizing and cataloging. Little did I know that this work would be laying the groundwork for a future foray into social entrepreneurship—based on my later efforts to help applicants do inventories to create their own databases to be matched up with the specific criteria of the most random or common or obscure scholarships.

The most powerful lesson I learned from the experience of those seven and a half months was to write down everything and anything that came to mind about what made me different. Ironically, as the geek who got bullied for being different, I realized that those differences I once saw as disadvantages were now the traits and attributes that made me unique. It turns out that differences like these—whatever is unique to your own life—are what makes you YOU and makes you special. These differences also line up, incredibly, with the specific criteria that many scholarship sources are looking for. Are you, for instance, the daughter of a single mother who is the first in the family to go to college, plays chess, and rides horses? I was not, although I was the son of a single mother who was the first in his family to go to college and was passionate about financial literacy, entrepreneurship, and leadership—and there were more than a few scholarships with those criteria.

Other spreadsheets for data I had been categorizing focused on the different types of essay prompts and questions that recurred frequently, along with roughly worded responses that could be fleshed out into longer essay submissions. The categories for most of the required essays came under the following headings I established:

1. Leadership
2. Community
3. Goals, both short- and long-term
4. Academics (favorite classes, strongest subjects)
5. Pursuit of knowledge (learning outside the classroom)

When I showed my essay spreadsheet with prompts and at least eight separate essays included on it, Ms. Holloway was shocked. She knew that I was only able to get onto a computer in her lab for an hour every night, along with whatever extra time I could get at the public library. When

I showed her the essays I had written on my phone (some of which I had already used for submissions), she was incredulous. Many students figure this out on their own, but few of us are told that you really only need to write three or four basic essays that you can freely adapt for different applications.

The content that I hoped would help me stand out was my response to the question of my long-term goals and my vision for creating two organizations: a nonprofit called the Financial Literacy Institute to teach underprivileged communities about doing more than making ends meet and actually accruing wealth, and a venture capital firm called Golden Bridge Investments. (I loved that name!) The key phrase I'd jotted down was "These long-term goals have stemmed from past financial adversities I have overcome and my ardent desire to serve and better society."

With technical guidance from Ms. Holloway and the emotionally grounding "keep the faith" reassurance from Dr. Starks, I was in good shape. Well, almost. The writing of my essays, I suspected, could use a review from someone who had expertise and who was willing to take the time to make sure my writing was in the realm of what was sought. I had no way of knowing.

No sooner had I realized that expertise was needed than I had a "best of times" experience. The exact right mentor entered my life in the form of my AP Literature teacher, Ms. Tara Tidwell, at the start of my senior year.

Every now and then you might be lucky enough to have a teacher like Ms. Tidwell who will not just prep you to get top scores on your AP Lit test but change how you understand and employ the written word. Her influence would be lasting. Ms. Tidwell knew that I couldn't afford a tutor or any paid help to review my scholarship or college application essays. Her door was open to me after her last class every afternoon. In the fall of 2009, I was in there almost on a daily basis. She would have me rewrite and sometimes restructure my essays, and then question a sentence here and there or encourage me to add details I'd forgotten. Ms. Tidwell became one more voice of reassurance that all would be well.

"Your story is on the page," she would say, and then proceed to suggest a series of improvements. Her suggestions were about clarity—making sure each essay had a coherent beginning, middle, and end. She encouraged me to grab the attention of the reviewers by including rich vocabulary words (like "perspicacity," one of my favorites). More than anything, her advice was to describe experiences that had taught me a revelatory lesson. My story of growing up in poverty and realizing I could turn misfortune into fortune for myself and for others was one I knew how to tell—at least the early part of it.

Nobody was as eager for me to get to go away to college than Ms. Tidwell. She herself had stayed in Alabama to receive her undergraduate and master's degrees from

Jacksonville State University, but she had then gone on to study British literature at the graduate level at Oxford University in England. With a wry sense of humor and boundless energy, Ms. Tidwell, who was white, didn't come from a background anywhere close to mine, yet in her AP class she managed to get me as excited as she was about stories of people and places completely removed from my experience. She later wrote about her profession as a teacher leader, saying, "Working with students means I can never do enough, know my subject enough, guide enough, foster independence enough . . . there is always more to do."

It was through Ms. Tidwell and AP Lit that I was exposed to Ralph Waldo Emerson, who is most often cited as the author of the words that would inspire my own book title years later: "Do not go where the path may lead. Go instead where there is no path and leave a trail." Those words were never actually found in any of his published works, although they strongly reflect Emerson's philosophy. Ms. Tidwell, who closely followed Emerson's writings, noted in her teacher's statement that she cared most about her students' intellectual growth and independence of thought. She pointed out that in "Self-Reliance," Emerson had said, "Nothing is at last sacred but the integrity of our own mind. Absolve you to yourself, and you shall have the suffrage of the world." Along those lines, she made it her mission to be an example of the power of lifelong learning.

The idea of becoming a lifelong learner freed me up to

write a winning scholarship essay in response to a prompt asking how I had acquired knowledge outside of the classroom:

> My journey of knowledge began on October 31, 1991 when I arrived in this world. My tiny red fists were clenched, my legs were wiggling, and my crying was probably heard throughout the emergency room. This was my first encounter with knowledge, and at the moment it took me by my hand and led me on an endless expedition toward intellectual excellence. I believe knowledge is a tool that is constantly sharpened and polished by experiences and the senses. Therefore, I am a life-long learner, an individual learning from everything he sees, feels, reads, tastes, and experiences. This means that in my intellectual pursuits I take the form of a scholar, a philosopher, an astronomer, or even a simple observer. At birth I was an observer, absorbing knowledge from my environment like a sponge and implementing what I learned through my actions.

After describing my life as the son of a young single mom, and telling of having to learn to teach myself basic life skills and then how to read and write on my own, I recounted how I sought wisdom and my own moral compass from life itself and from the Bible, which had inspired me to use the knowledge I gained for the good of humanity.

Finally, I cataloged the storehouses of knowledge to be gained from oral histories of other people, as well as in a range of media, from video games to comic books to literary classics. I concluded:

> My pursuit of knowledge will be a perpetual journey. I will continue to learn each day from my senses, books, adversities, and other aspects of life. Knowledge will continue to mold my persona and spearhead me into adulthood and carry me to excellence in my college education.

Ms. Tidwell, like my other mentors, was as generous to my fellow students as she was to me. We all knew her door was open to us, anytime. She loved all kinds of writing and made it her goal for us, as she would say, "to love fiction for the suspension of one's belief, to love poetry for its music, to love grammar for its style, and to love nonfiction for the language that explains math and science." Over the course of AP Lit, I did fall in love with every genre of the written word that Ms. Tidwell put on her syllabus and into my hands.

The classic works we read and dissected included everything from Shakespeare's *Hamlet* to Milton's *Paradise Lost*, from Mary Shelley's *Frankenstein* to Oscar Wilde's *Picture of Dorian Grey*. I felt Hamlet's struggle "to be or not to be" and learned from the play about love and the consequences of jealousy and revenge. Wilde's *Dorian Grey* was just a compelling page-turner, not to mention that it dealt with the complexities of human psychology—always an area of interest to me. For different reasons, both *Frankenstein* and *Paradise Lost* appealed to me in my quest for spiritual wisdom. Each had something different to say about our relationship with our Creator and the limits of our powers as human beings and our God-given free will.

Later on, in hearing the accounts of tech start-ups that were conceived in dorm rooms as the result of friendly contests or even dares, I would recall being captivated by the story of how eighteen-year-old Mary Wollstonecraft Godwin Shelley conceived of her novel after agreeing to a friendly competition with her husband, Percy Shelley, and their friend Lord Byron who proposed they compete to see who could write the best horror tale. A short time later, as the story went, Mary had a terrifying dream about a scientist who created a man in his laboratory who turned out to be a monster. She put her dream onto the page to write *Frankenstein; or, The Modern Prometheus,* as she subtitled it, drawing from the Greek myth that told of the stealing of fire from the gods. Her horror novel's opening epigraph paid homage to Milton with a quote from *Paradise Lost.*

In class discussion and in my one-on-one conversations with Ms. Tidwell, I was fascinated by questions that came up about the unfettered power of the internet and the ability to access information at lightning speed. For instance, without moral constraints, what would keep the overlords of the tech and financial worlds from taking over? After Ms. Tidwell picked up on my growing interest in the famous tech entrepreneurs of Silicon Valley and the big-name financial wizards of Wall Street, she began to recommend nonfiction books and articles about leadership in the modern era.

Her first suggestion was Malcolm Gladwell's *Outliers*— which was close to a life-changing experience for me. The things that made me feel different, I had already learned, were what also made me unique. But the concept of being an outlier explained a lot to me about myself. From all that Gladwell revealed, outliers are the least likely by conventional standards to succeed, yet the most likely to have significant outlier types of success. Similarly, when I read *Blink* and *The Tipping Point*, his earlier books, I understood better how I processed information and how trends can collide with events in ways that matter in business and in society.

To my frustration, there were no major memoirs at the time of Bill Gates, Steve Jobs, Elon Musk, or Jeff Bezos. There were magazine features, of course, and I soaked those up, not just for the articles on Silicon Valley VIPs but also for stories about famous African-American entrepreneurs. One of my later Black business heroes was someone whose name first crossed my path in these years. Robert F.

Smith—raised in a middle-class family in Denver, the son of two educators—had an inspiring story of using his undergrad degree from Cornell in chemical engineering and an MBA from Columbia to rise up in the ranks at Goldman Sachs, where he made a name for himself in technology investment banking and in mergers and acquisitions. In 2000, Robert F. Smith founded his own company, Vista Equity Partners, a Silicon Valley and private equity firm that was changing the face, if not the color, of the tech world. Later he would establish a philanthropic arm of his company and devote a good share of his fortune to scholarships and help pay off the college debt of students at historically Black colleges and universities.

As an almost eighteen-year-old, the emerging dream I had for myself still included the possibility of working in high-level finance, but increasingly I could see myself one day branching off in an entrepreneurial capacity. There was no one out there who looked like me—no Black Bill Gates. At least not yet. I kept searching and looking, keeping my nose to the ground.

Thanks to reading suggested by all three of my mentors—Ms. Tidwell, Ms. Holloway, and Dr. Starks—I started to collect and archive inspirational quotes that helped fortify my faith that all would be well, no matter which turn I took on my ever-uncertain path.

My favorite quote, and one I used in a few of my essays, was by author Elaine Maxwell, a health-care specialist.

Her words gave me a self-defining mantra that helped me slug it out in the last couple months of getting all my scholarship submissions in as I prepared to apply to college: "My will shall shape my future. Whether I fail or succeed shall be no man's doing but my own. I am the force; I can clear any obstacle before me or I can be lost in the maze. My choice; my responsibility; win or lose, only I hold the key to my destiny."

It may sound banal, but that mantra, combined with a system and a Bruce Wayne–like regimen to learn the equations of the dreaded AP Calculus, got me through the class and kept my GPA intact.

My Big Ma knew nothing about calculus, but when I reported to her that I had faced my big challenge, she could not have been more proud.

In your own version of "the best of times and the worst of times," the self-defining moments are the ones when you get to choose which times will get the better of you and which will bring out the best in you. You'll see shortly why focusing on how to *use what you don't have* can lead you to *receive what you would like to have.*

Without giving away all the specifics of what was about to happen, I realize now that in Bruce Wayne fashion, I had made a science out of applying for scholarships. At the heart of that effort, of course, was writing the essays. Some of the pointers I can offer include the suggestion that if you're given an "optional" prompt, *do* it. Just consider it mandatory and go the distance. Overperform in every way you can.

Make sure not to rush or leave essays for the last minute so that you have time to really show the multidimensional aspects of yourself in writing an essay that gives a portrait of you that can't be reflected in just your GPA or test scores. Don't make the mistake of meandering from the prompt. Stick to it but don't repeat it word for word. You want to be clear and concise and show intellectual depth. If the prompt is asking about a time when you achieved something despite a setback, don't write about what you'll do with the scholarship money if you win. If you're asked to discuss what you want to study in college and why, don't write about the day your baby sister was born (unless that directly pertains to your college and career goals!). Try to avoid redundancy in your essay—that is, don't narrate accomplishments already listed in your academic/work résumé.

Stay within the word count. Follow the rules for narrative structure, but remember that you are not writing an academic essay. If you can be funny or move a reader close to tears, go ahead. That is powerful writing. If you can offer an authentic view others may not have considered, go for it. A shortcoming that we hear reviewers mention often is that scholarship and admission essays don't follow the rule of "show, don't tell."

If you're asked to describe one of your proudest moments, don't just say that it was winning the election for student council president, but vividly describe the details of running a campaign, the challenge of coming up with a platform, and your feelings before and after the vote was in.

In yet one more installment of "do as I say, not as I did," below are a few more tips that I learned over the course of applying for well over fifty scholarships. Had I done a slightly better job at tracking those applications—which I really encourage you to do—I could give you an exact number.

It also has occurred to me that some of the practices that worked for me in hunting and applying for scholarships can also be used in the college admissions search and application process, in a job hunt, and even in the development of branding materials for your start-up. Or maybe—and this is a leap, but check it out—these practices can be a template for your own dating approach, for finding the kind of person you might want to date.

As much as I love technology for making notes, I recommend going back to ancient times by keeping a physical notebook handy for jotting down thoughts and answers. You can always transfer your notes to a spreadsheet, Word doc, or other format for keeping organized.

However you choose to chronicle your efforts, doing so will be a reward in itself and a reminder in the future of how you ventured onto a path of your own making. Tools to help along the way include:

1. Create a List of Your Unique Traits

What special, distinctive, compelling, or other unique attributes do you have to offer? This is powerful information whatever you may be searching for. When it comes to scholarships, jobs, investors, and more, they are out there looking for you. My search for scholarships brought my attention to specifics that funders are looking for: nationality, personal interests, GPA, languages spoken, extracurricular activities, and diverse family histories. There are scholarships for swimmers, pianists, fantasy football players, students who grew up with certain hardships, first-generation college students, LGBTQ+ individuals, and so on.

Categories to get you going are:

- Personal interests and passions

- Extracurricular activities

- Hardships you or your family have endured (for example, cancer, loss of a parent, a natural disaster)

- Career interests or goals

- Academic accomplishments/interests/awards

- Heritage

- Personality traits (for example, strong sense of leadership, great sense of humor)

This inventory will remind you that colleges, scholarships, jobs, investors, and even potential dates are looking for *you*. This will also help keep you from taking a shotgun approach—applying for everything, whatever it is. Apply for opportunities that are a fit for you.

2. Let Your Traits Be Your Guide in Your Search for Opportunity

In addition to the more obvious opportunities—such as the high-competition scholarships available through the Gates Millennium Scholars Program and the Ronald McDonald House Charities—there are thousands of other scholarships and other kinds of opportunities often overlooked by others that take more legwork but may be the right fit for you. If you are applying to college or grad school, look beyond the familiar names. If you are switching careers and feel overqualified for starting over, look for employers who value experience. There are many of us—including my company—who look for diversity in our hires, including age diversity. "There is a lid to every pot" is an expression that's used by professional dating matchmakers. Look for opportunity that matches your uniqueness.

3. Develop a Prioritized List of Opportunities

Get organized. Keep a flowchart that keeps you on task. For scholarships, you'll want a list that prioritizes due date, unique fit, and scholarship amount. Obviously, top priority should be given to those with the closest approaching deadlines, followed by the type of scholarship (how uniquely it matches you) and then the dollar amount. The same approach can be implemented for your other searches. What do you need to do and when?

This should go without saying, but it's important to take your time reading instructions and to follow them to a tee. Then keep a log of what applications you sent and when, and what responses you received.

4. Cast a Wide Net for Opportunity

The conventional advice for college applicants is to have three categories of institutions—*reach* (the most competitive colleges), *target* (competitive but where you see yourself earning admissions), and *safety* (less competitive and a backup in case you don't get into your preferred choices). Unfortunately, I never applied to any of the private schools that require additional financial records that cost money to fill out and that charge additional application fees. Later I'd learn that those fees could have been waived, even though there would have been other hoops to jump through. A lesson I learned was not to limit myself, and you shouldn't either. Apply for as many scholarships as possible, and go big and competitive. But don't dismiss smallish scholarships either. There are tons out there in the $500–$2,000 range, and they add up. Trust me.

You can apply the wisdom of casting a wide net for opportunity as a life mantra. Get yourself on a schedule, however. Every day make sure you are casting one more line out into the ocean of opportunity that awaits you.

5. Build an Opportunity "Toolbox" (and Save Time Later)

What, you might ask, is an opportunity toolbox? Basically, it's a repository of the resources, materials, info, and knowledge you'll need to slay your search and application process, whatever it is. An opportunity toolbox works for scholarships, college applications, job hunting, investor searches, and yes, even for dating. By gathering all of the (potentially) necessary items and information you'll need *ahead of time*, you'll be able to work more efficiently, cover more ground in less time, and again, cast a wide net. There are items to consider accumulating well in advance of needing them. For example, some parents start a "brag file" early in their child's life that includes honors, awards, memberships, press, letters of praise, and photography from special occasions.

Other items to consider:

- Letters of recommendation

- CVs

- Job résumés

- Professional bios

- Personal statements or college essays you've written in the past

- Academic records and transcripts

- Financial forms and reports like the FAFSA/SAR report and the CSS profile

- Any loan documents

- Parents' tax returns if relevant

- Traditional/professional-looking headshots

- College board IDs

- Links to press or sites like LinkedIn (it's advisable even for high school students to list part-time jobs or summer internships)

- Social media links (making sure that you have cleaned up and deleted anything that shows you in an unfavorable light)

For anyone about to go where there is no path, creating an opportunity toolbox is an act of self-empowerment.

Probably one of my life's most important lessons came to me in this time of uncertainty when things were happening far outside of my control. I couldn't fix the economy or make sure my mother got a job again. All I could control was how I responded to the uncertainty and how I took action to do my part to improve my chances at being able to afford the education I so passionately wanted.

Having given it my absolute all, the only thing left to do was wait in faith.

In the winter of 2009–2010, I had not yet heard back from any of the groups and foundations whose scholarships I'd applied for. My college applications had gone in without a lot of effort. In hindsight, I should have probably applied to some Ivy schools (like Penn), and I wish I had known, or had tried to find out, that they waive application fees in cases of financial need. At a certain point, however, once Drexel and Philadelphia had fixed themselves in my vision, the other colleges where I applied were more like placeholders in case for some reason I didn't get into Drexel.

Still, from an affordability standpoint, I was nervous to be putting all the eggs in that basket. No full ride was going to happen necessarily.

In the meantime, there were still AP tests to study for. I was in the library studying quietly one afternoon when I heard my phone buzz in my pocket and grabbed it without realizing who the call was from.

In a cheerful voice, an executive introduced himself as being part of the Horatio Alger Scholarship organization, and he followed up quickly to say, "Congratulations, you have been selected as the recipient . . ."

The rest of his words blurred until he got to the award amount. For a second I thought I had heard wrong when he said, "Twenty thousand dollars." But, no, he repeated that same amount, explaining that it would be in addition to any financial aid I received from wherever I was given an admissions offer.

I jumped up from my chair, speechless. In tears.

I couldn't help myself. Twenty thousand dollars was almost half of what I was going to need to pay for my first year of college. That, together with what I hoped to receive in financial aid, meant that *IT WAS REAL! I WAS GOING AWAY TO COLLEGE!* Had my ship come in? Or just a rowboat? It didn't matter. I was ecstatic!

Ms. Holloway came over as soon as I hung up. When I told her, half crying, half laughing, she started to cry. I never thought that I could feel that happy again.

Oh, but I could. The next notification was from the Coca-Cola Foundation. Their award was also $20,000—and included a trip to Atlanta to join up with other award recipients. Barely able to speak on that phone call, I asked in a daze, "How do I get to Atlanta?" Somehow I thought that I had to go there to pick up the award. No, I was re-assured, they would fly me there, and the award money would go to the bursar's office wherever I chose to attend.

If those had been the only awards, it would have still been everything. But there was more. A lot more. The day that I heard from the Bill and Melinda Gates Foundation will forever remain a blur in my memory. The notification arrived in the mail. When I opened it, I was half expecting to read a kindly worded rejection explaining that there had been a deluge of worthy applicants, but that they wished me well and all that stuff.

That was not what happened. The recipient named on the notification was none other than Christopher Gray. I did fall to my knees in prayer and thanks.

There were more, mightily cherished awards—from places like the Mensa Foundation, whose directors are highly selective and who honored me as one of their own. When all was said and done, I'd received thirty-four schol-arship awards, comprising multiple full rides, and I was going to be able not only to afford four years of college but also go on for a master's and a PhD, if I so chose.

By the time I graduated from high school, I had become

known as the Million Dollar Scholar. To be more exact, I was a $1.3 million multi-scholarship winner.

Against many odds, I had achieved my dream of going as far away as I could to college, and yes, I was accepted by Drexel University, where I intended to go for a double major in entrepreneurship and finance. Two months after graduation, for my very first purchase out of my scholarship winnings, I bought a plane ticket—one way—and packed everything I owned into one suitcase.

In a hurry, I made a round of good-byes to relatives and friends. A wave of nostalgia came over me as I went by Ramsay High School, but not enough to keep me on the island. Leaving my two younger siblings, ages two and three, was hard, though.

This had been a complicated time between Momma and me. The irony was that it was my mom—forced to hustle to survive in her life—who had told me if there was something I wanted to have or do, then it was up to me to make it happen. She was undeniably proud of me, yet for some reason, maybe because she couldn't relate, she seemed to resent the whole subject of my going away to college.

On the morning she was supposed to drive me to the airport, as we'd planned, Momma said, a couple of hours before we'd planned to leave, "Christopher, you gonna have to get yourself another ride."

Just like that. No apology. No explanation.

Deep down I knew she was avoiding the hurt of saying

good-bye. But at the time, I was crushed. When I called Dr. Starks, she graciously offered to drop everything, come pick me up, and take me to the airport.

"If it's inconvenient, I could call a cab."

"Not at all," she insisted, saying this would give us a chance to discuss my academic program. She knew I would be nervous, but did all she could to keep things light.

The first time I'd ever flown on an airplane had been that trip to Atlanta and back by myself, for the gathering of the Coca-Cola scholarship winners. Talk about a trip. No exaggeration, flying freaked me out! For only my third trip, I was now flying to a city and a campus I'd visited only briefly before committing. I'd be living in Philadelphia for the next five years, and I didn't know a single person there.

At the airport, Dr. Starks walked me toward the line for security and cheerfully waved me on. "Go get 'em," she laughed and turned to go before I could respond.

Today I fly all the time and think nothing of it. Not then. I can still see myself and how overwhelmed I was boarding the flight to Philly, and how, not long after takeoff, I leaned over to glance out of the plane's small window for a last look at the Magic City fading far below me. We were already in the clouds. That's when I realized—almost fearfully—that I was free.

I pulled down the window shade and never looked back. Going home, back to the island, even for a visit, became harder and harder after that day.

It had never really occurred to me before that there were so many others like me trying to get off their islands too. Ships do come in, and I was proof of that.

Clearly, some kind of ship had come in. Was it all going to be smooth sailing from here? No, that wouldn't be realistic. All I knew was that things were going to work out.

Faith is the transformative force of good that we can all access when we choose, I promise. Choose to give it a try when you step out into the unknown. Meet the present moment with anticipation that you are going to find a way—and you will.

You really will.

Once you are in motion, going where there is no path, the next part is the place where all the action and adventure happens. There you just might get to leave a trail for others, and have your cake and eat it too.

Chapter 6

The Product Is Still King

CONCEIVING AND CREATING SCHOLLY

I don't like to solve new needs. I like to solve existing needs.

—Josh Kopelman, entrepreneur, venture
capitalist, inventor, philanthropist, chairman of the board
of Philadelphia Media Network

We started our whole conversation, as you may recall, with the question that's invariably asked of tech entrepreneurs and founders of digital start-ups: *How does it feel when you hit upon an idea that makes so much sense it stops you in your tracks?*

You may remember my description of how that happened when I had my big aha! moment in the spring of my third year at Drexel University. Again, those inflection points have always felt to me like a Call to Action, or a nudge from the universe.

The experience may be felt differently by each of us,

without a doubt. Although, when I've talked this over with friends and peers and fellow founders, they've each described similar reactions. For most of us, the moment registers like having that proverbial light bulb turn on in the dark room of our minds. True. Whenever you've been mulling over a problem or trying to come up with a solution or a tangible product that supplies an answer to a need, it is a lot like banging around in the dark where others have tried and failed to achieve a workable solution.

This experience isn't reserved just for folks who are product developers or who are trying to get in on the online tech economy. Whenever you are pushing yourself in the direction of where you'd like to be headed next and aren't sure how to go about it, you most likely are bound to spend time trying to mentally figure it out—either in solitary detective style or by tapping the thoughts of friends, family, advisers, mentors, therapists, and others. You may even chat with strangers on the bus or with Uber drivers.

The feedback you get may help you understand all the other ways that we are all in need of innovation.

Maybe, in an academic setting, you're eager to thrive and stand out and you've got to come up with original content and a powerful thesis. When the answer comes to you, it is a golden moment that can spur you on your way. Or let's look at a financial challenge, which can be personal, business-related, or a concern that affects a lot of people: *How am I (are we) going to pay for __ [fill in the blank]?*

Your back could be against the wall, and that might force you to find a solution and flip on the light switch fast. Or what about those times in your career when you have an opportunity to walk through a door (or get on a Zoom call) and deliver a pitch or an edgy strategy? Your concept, especially if it's in response to a pressing problem others have recognized or a product or service that could help the company's bottom line, could be the key to your future success.

We've all heard the saying that necessity is the mother of invention. I would add, so too is opportunity.

Taking these hypotheticals even further, let's say that your unmarked path has inspired you to envision building a company of your own and you've been trying to do so by conceiving of a product or service or brand identity that will set you apart; hopefully it will do so by offering a solution to a problem that needs solving. In this scenario, you're possibly hoping that whatever you've got going can attract investment to give you starting capital for your company and that it can be monetized on an ongoing basis.

This may sound like an inversion of the more organic way that big ideas are commonly thought to arise first from the need to solve a problem—a need made even more urgent and purposeful if it has personally impacted you. Take the oldest, most celebrated invention said to have revolutionized the world—the printing press. Johannes Gutenberg, a German goldsmith, is known to have come up with the idea and technology for this machine as a solution to the problem of how long it took to print just one Bible by hand. How could he think of a way to get the Word of God as chronicled in the Bible into more places and more quickly? The printing press, you could say, could well have been divinely inspired.

How else, otherwise, could the Christian-Judeo teachings have been spread so far, so rapidly? Simply put, the printing press was the tipping point that led to the end of the Dark Ages and the acceleration of the Renaissance, making it possible to reproduce greater numbers of texts (religious and otherwise) in a shorter amount of time. The global spread of knowledge was now possible.

As the story goes, the idea to mass-produce the printed word had come to Gutenberg after he observed a machine that could manufacture large numbers of the small mirrors that people wore on their clothes when they went to visit holy places. Fortunately, Gutenberg had technical skills from having worked at a coin mint, and so he was able to apply his understanding of mechanization to develop the printing press. He began with a practical, simple question and came up with a practical, straightforward solution—a product that changed the world forevermore.

Most of us generally know that much, although there are aspects to the story that don't get mentioned too often. First, why did he care so much about reproducing the Bible? Apparently, the driving motivation for Gutenberg was that he was desperate for money and wanted to find something highly desirable and valued that he could sell in great numbers. So the lesson is that *there is nothing wrong with looking for an idea that can make you a lot of money.* And there's also nothing wrong with evaluating an idea's viability based on whether or not *it solves a problem* and whether or not *that solution is commercial.* Gutenberg was trying to solve a problem in 1436 or thereabouts, and he wasn't so different from anyone today who wants to get in on the tech industry and then tries to give birth to ideas that will create a supply for a demand. Hustle, after all, is really the mother of invention.

The other point that gets overlooked is that what made the Gutenberg Bible a contender for the number-one invention of the last millennium was this: its inventor understood the number-one principle that I had to learn, through trial and error: *product is king.*

People continually try to say that this is no longer true and that marketing is equally as important as the product itself, if not more so. I would argue otherwise. Marketing is extremely important, but product is still king.

Sure, there are definitely other elements to turning your idea into a business reality and your solution into monetary success. Finding the right funders and partners is one of those elements. In the example of Johannes Gutenberg, the History Channel looked at the printing press and underscored its inventor's awareness that product is king, pointing out how meticulous he was in his choice of design and the colors of illustrations and the mastery of the printing of the different versions of the Bible. This show also noted, sadly, how Gutenberg lost ownership of his invention:

> Gutenberg's business partner Johann Fust sued him for the return of a large sum of money loaned to help in the production of his Bibles. Gutenberg lost the lawsuit, and the final ruling stipulated that he had to turn his printing equipment and half the completed Bibles over to Fust, who went on to peddle them along with one of Gutenberg's former assistants, Peter Schoeffer. Gutenberg was driven into financial ruin.

Fewer than two hundred Gutenberg Bibles were ever printed, and a little over forty exist today. The going price for just one of them would be $35 million at current market value.

None of this cautionary tale should sound foreign to anyone who has had their Call to Action moment but then went on to stumble in the *execution* of turning a great idea into phenomenal content or an amazing product or system of service.

That's why, once you've heard the Call, your follow-up most logical question should be: *What's next? How can I protect my concept? How can I make it happen?* As my mentors taught me, the best way to protect your idea is to build it with proprietary and protected methods, although there are other considerations we'll discuss up ahead.

Obviously, if it's an idea to write something—a story, an article, a book, a movie—go get busy. If it's something you are ready to present in a safe setting where what you're presenting will belong to your employer, you can get to work on your presentation. Legally, your employer can't steal your idea from you if you've been developing it on their dime. Generally, they own it. Still, if you can claim credit for its development, do so, and if you have collaborators, give them credit too.

If, on the other hand, you're going full-on entrepreneur with your idea, you've got real work to do in bringing that idea to life with some kind of prototype before you show it to anyone. It's so important to do your homework and learn as much as you can about how others have successfully approached the development and marketing of this type of product. Information you'll want to seek out includes such questions as how others have protected their intellectual property and what measures were taken to collaborate successfully with partners.

Intellectual property law is something that impacts almost all of us, even when we're not actively trying to come up with an invention or our own product or company. It's important to know not just how to protect your original material, in whatever form, but also how to protect yourself from accusations of theft by others.

In the Wild Wild West of the internet, where everyone is always quoting, posting, creating memes, adding music, and sharing content, there are few rules that users know to follow. So, there's good news and there's bad news. If you are promoting yourself or selling something, the good news, up to a point, is that social media offers a bonanza of free advertising. When you can hit that sweet spot and offer something that gives you a platform, you can gain traction. The bad news is that you can also gain imitators and competitors. That's why it's so important to protect yourself from being overexposed.

Not to be overly dramatic, but in my experience there are scoundrels and thieves hiding in plain sight wherever ideas can be monetized. They are notorious in the entertainment and tech worlds, but they should be better recognized in most every business setting. Sometimes thieves don't even know they're stealing. This is why, as I had to learn, developing your brand identity is crucial. Think about it—when you've branded your material or product, it's aligned with you, and that makes it harder to steal. Just remember, though: it's the product that matters even more than the brand.

Maybe someone happens to hear you float a concept you're just developing, and that person goes off and tweaks it and makes it a slightly different concept, and now, sorry, but they've developed an interesting product. In this scenario, you really aren't protected in any way. That's why it's good to keep your cards close to your vest until you have developed your idea enough that it would be objectively obvious to anyone if someone else outright copies it.

Common sense reminds us that if you are an idea person or aspire to be an innovator, a tech developer, or an original content creator, it's highly advisable to investigate what you might need in order to protect your project from theft. A few basics you can explore include:

1. Whether or not you should ask someone to sign a nondisclosure agreement before you share the details of a project with them
2. How to secure the copyright on original content you create, like works of fiction, comic books, music, screenplays, etc.
3. When you might need legal or business advice on obtaining trademarks (logos, designs, symbols, or other identifiers of branded content) and patents (to protect a range of inventions in tech, science, medicine and more)

There is a category in intellectual property law that includes what are known as "trade secrets," which you want to be sure to protect with whatever resources you can find. For one thing, if your app, for example, uses technology that is based on a proprietary algorithm, that adds enormous value when you go out looking for investors. This value can be reflected in high-level research, data studies, or trade secrets for production processes—like a specific formula or special chemical that creates a higher demand for a product. For another thing, when you have a trade secret that is protected, it tells others that your developed idea is that much harder to steal. Because it's *secret*!

Here's an interesting lesson that came my way once I got to college. Much to my surprise, when I combined hood wisdom with everything I could learn in an academic setting, it was soon evident that one of the best ways to differentiate an idea from those of other people is to think about the same questions used for college and scholarship essays: *What's my story? What sets me apart? How do my goals and dreams fit with the foundation's parameters or the institution's goals?* In other words: *What sets my idea apart, and how can I tell that story?* When you're ready to go out and get buy-in, you can address questions that come from others: *How does my idea/product/company align with the goals of investors or employers?* When you are trying to reach customers or an audience for your products as an entrepreneur, the questions continue to be similar: *How does what I'm marketing solve a concern or add value to the lives of the greatest number of people?* Taking it one step further, as a social entrepreneur, you might ask: *How does my company seek to address existing problems facing society as a whole?*

None of these protections and questions guarantees you

a successful outing the first time you decide to take your idea off the drawing board of your imagination and turn it into a marketable product or other entity.

And so, as the wisest leaders in the field will tell you, *be prepared to fail*—but be equally prepared to *learn the lesson from that failure and how not to repeat it*. Be prepared for rejection and competition too, on whatever turf you're staking out while going along on your unconventional path.

My reasons for emphasizing all of this should become clearer up ahead.

Over the first three of my five years of college in Philadelphia, I went through a series of rude awakenings and eye-opening experiences. That's as it should be, I guess, as a part of the growing-up process and what's meant to happen in your college years. Maybe I should have done even more of that. There have been moments when I've regretted not carving time out for more of a social life. Doing so would have allowed me to decompress from the high school pressure that had built up just trying to get into college and hustling to afford it.

By the way, this pattern is excruciatingly common. It's something that I would later address in writing and in coaching about how to avoid burnout *before* you start college and how to keep a balance while adjusting to an environment very different from the one you left behind.

It's normal to be thrown off-balance while going through the culture shock or the free-for-all that many experience during their first year away from home.

My situation being what it was, however, from the moment I moved into my dorm I resolved not to party, and not even to drink on occasion, for fear that it would jeopardize my good standing. I applied this resolution not just at Drexel but also at Penn, where I spent many hours on special entrepreneurship programs connected to both business schools. Being in good standing had mattered all my life, but now it was attached to ongoing financial support from scholarship providers.

Sometimes I question my own extreme measures. College camaraderie and fun are necessary rites of passage, and that's why, for today's students, I would say to make sure you are not so driven and so serious that you miss out. Hopefully you will be able to enjoy your college years before you face the demands of the real world. Not only that, but take advantage of learning opportunities and explorations you may not be able to pursue later on. Definitely, I regret not taking more classes that were outside my double majors of finance and entrepreneurship; I regret feeling the need to be so careful.

My advice to you—to be classified as "do not as I did, but as others have successfully done"—would be to follow the instructions of the late Steve Jobs, cofounder of Apple, who famously said, "Stay hungry, stay foolish."

That was his advice for going where the path doesn't lead—because vision is sparked by being hungry for something bigger and better that only exists off the beaten track. What's more, it's because the act of creating a new solution to an old problem is so much likelier to happen when you're willing to throw caution to the wind or even be downright impractical.

Hungry I was. But maybe not foolish enough.

My thinking went like this: *If I blow it and, God forbid, flunk out or have to go home, there's nowhere at home to hunker down and reboot.* Some of my more privileged friends might have had to take time off from too much foolishness, but they had families and financial support to help them get back on track.

Bottom line, for better and for worse, I always had to be the grown-up in the room. It was part of my training. Still, many of my ruder awakenings came when I realized I'd lived for so long in a narrow-minded place and had preconceived ideas of how the world works. I know that this too is not so unique. So much so that I would say, if you go away to attain the best education possible and you don't have your thinking or your assumptions challenged, you have missed out on the gift that college gives us of expanding our worldly knowledge and wisdom.

Culture shock can actually be a good thing. When you go from the highly segregated hood to a private university with cultural and geographic diversity—and an enrollment of over 25,000 students with minorities in the minority—that's a shock. Many of my new friends were white, and others were from Black, Latinx, Asian, immigrant, and other ethnically and culturally diverse backgrounds. Generally, because many of my peers came from more progressive homes and places, there was a pronounced acceptance of openly LGBTQ+ students. It was a breath of fresh air in contrast to the taboos that I'd experienced in the Bible Belt of Alabama, particularly in the African-American community, where some were still beating the gay out of family members.

At home I'd been a bigger fish in a small pond of 98 percent students of color who were academically high-achieving, and more than half of whom were raised in economically challenged households. Very few people in my high school who were LGBTQ+ were known to be so, to the best of my knowledge. That may have been the reason I didn't come out until I was a senior at Drexel. For me, there was no dramatic rite of passage where you sit your family down and give them the news. Instead, I remember a friend asking if I was dating one of the more sought-after gay men on campus, and I stated, "We're talking." Then I laughed and acknowledged we were seeing each other. That was it.

Dr. Starks, who regularly kept in touch, was someone I did tell after that, and her response was "I thought that you'd come to that conclusion, Chris, but it was important for you to get there in your own way and in your own time." She was happy for me, she said, because I had an opportunity—by being open about it—to make someone else's process of coming out easier.

This meant, as a Black, gay Millennial who was contemplating a future in finance and/or as an entrepreneur, I was even more of an outlier. There was no role model or exemplar of those traits who had left a trail for someone like me. But I wasn't concerned. Somehow I felt certain that I would find the right allies at the right time and that the right doors would open.

Whatever may be your perceived disadvantages, I want you to know they can also be the same distinctive traits that get you noticed, that can be assets, and that give you a competitive edge, connecting you to motivated people who hold values common to your own. Never once did I regret being anything other than fully out and proud to be who I am in every respect.

The atmosphere of acceptance at a northeastern university in that regard was something I would always be grateful for. However, not everything about adjusting to the views of others was easy—to my surprise.

All that time I spent in a place with a Smallville mentality (I know, now we're switching to another superhero story), I can remember thinking, once I got to the "Metropolis" and was able to do big things à la Clark Kent/ Superman, I'd shake loose that old feeling of not belonging.

After all those years of feeling that I was disconnected from the universe of cutting-edge ideas—with only faulty reception beaming in from outer space—I assumed that the people up north would be evolved and like-minded, and that I'd be leaving the sting of small-mindedness, racism, and classism behind.

That just goes to show how naive I was.

The truth is that racism exists in the North too, but, as others have pointed out, it's spoken with a different accent. In the South, there's not much artifice or apology, so the discrimination is more of a given, more out in the open. But there's prejudice in the North too, outside of those former Confederate strongholds, only it's usually more covert or subtle, and sometimes more systemic.

During my freshman year an offhanded comment took me by surprise while I was studying late at night at the computer lab, where I spent countless hours at Drexel. I got to talking to a fellow student who asked how I was doing in certain classes. I said, "Great."

No need for false modesty, I figured.

This included Entrepreneurship 101, the class that we all took if that was our major and that others took for its life strategies as well. We spent the first semester studying entrepreneurial thinking and the second semester learning the nuts and bolts of starting a company. This was my wheelhouse and I loved it. Apparently, this fellow student thought the class was hard, so he seemed impressed by how well I was doing.

"You know, you're different," he said. When I gave him a questioning look, he went on. "You're obviously very smart. You're not like most of the Black people I know."

He said that as if he thought I'd take it as a compliment. That was the problem. The implication was that other students of color or people of color he knew from where he grew up were not smart, goal-oriented, or hardworking like me. I may have given him a harsh look, but he didn't get it.

Other, similar remarks were not as clumsy as his, but they got to me. Sometimes I did feel the pressure to prove to them that Black people are more than our race and more than how we're portrayed on TV. And then I saw more closely that racism comes from how perceptions are ingrained over time—and how they become solidified in what's known as a racist mentality. So nothing I could do would necessarily change how they thought of other Black folks. They would only revert back to making me the exception.

That eye-opening did plant the seeds in me for a later understanding about how to more effectively confront systemic racism. Rather than try to tear down a pernicious system, why not build an alternative system that is led in more inclusive, more just, and more equitable ways? Of course, it wasn't my job to fix the system. My job was to say

YES to my own success and NO to validating ignorance. I do suspect, though, that close encounters with different kinds of racist ideologies fueled my developing belief that only by creating opportunity for ourselves—as owners, leaders, and influencers with true financial power—would we as people of color pave the way toward real economic justice. Looking at where ignorance is bred also informed my subsequent fight for equal access to quality education for *all*.

The other bit of culture shock that took me by surprise had to do with class divisions that I knew existed but had never really experienced up close.

Growing up, I hadn't really known a lot of people who were in any way privileged. In Philly, I had friends who were from families that came over on the *Mayflower* and who had been to private schools all their lives, as well as friends who came from middle- and upper-middle-class backgrounds. Then, of course, I had friends who, like me, couldn't have afforded college without scholarships, financial aid, and student loans. It was startling how people raised in privilege had so little understanding about the challenges faced by those of us who grew up poor. They wanted to be compassionate and concerned, but they couldn't relate. You'd hear everyone talking about their ski vacations certain times of the year, while scholarship students like me would be wondering if any of the dining halls were open on campus.

This was a rude awakening. I may have been the Million Dollar Scholar, but I didn't actually have $1.3 million handed to me to stick in my account. That money was earmarked for educational costs—from undergrad to grad school, through to a doctoral program and any postgrad courses in between. Most of my expenses were covered, but I had to request the funds. When I wasn't in class, like during holidays, I was on my own. I could request funds, under "special circumstances," to cover my needs during these times, but it wasn't like those funds were *my* money that I could tap anytime.

Dr. Starks had once told me that the famous phrase "you can't go home again" might apply to me. Over summers and vacations when I couldn't take classes or get internships in Philly, I tried going home. While it gave me a chance to see my younger siblings, my Big Ma, and my grandfather, my mother and I had our issues. After the first two years, I gave up and stayed in Philadelphia on campus. There was usually someone during holidays who was in the same boat as me, and we could go grab a meal together and work on our laptops in coffee shops and make do.

It was in that context that the conversation would frequently arise as to how the outside scholarship process worked for me. Often the bulk of scholarships are given for that first year; then comes your sophomore year when you're hit with a bill that you realize you don't know how you're going to pay. Financial aid offices at most institutions will help students identify additional loans to combine with the school's contribution for the year. More and more, though, we were hearing horror stories about ballooning interest rates on student loans and the inability of graduates to pay them off because of stagnant wages in the job market. I'd hear people talking about having to drop out of school and work for a while to earn enough in order to avoid accumulating debt. The more I heard about people feeling stuck, the more I saw how dysfunctional the system had become and wanted to be able to help.

That's when I'd go to my notes about scholarships offered for undergraduates already enrolled. Friends would look at me in amazement, as if I had found the Holy Grail. Some were skeptical—like this was a lottery or a crapshoot.

"Nope," I'd insist. "There's all this money looking for students that will go unclaimed if they don't get applicants that fit their terms."

Soon word got around that I had this database. If I could help friends (and friends of friends) in need of finding a scholarship or two, I would. Somebody would mention, say, that they played the saxophone and I'd remember a scholarship for horn instrument players, look it up in my notes, and give them the info. Before long I was a walking, living app without even intending to be one.

I certainly wasn't thinking of being a scholarship "app" as a goal; all I was doing was informally helping fellow students in need of money for staying in school. That was just being a helpful person, something I'd appreciate someone else doing for me if I didn't have the info.

Ironically, though, I did have apps on the brain.

Apps were the big buzz of the business and media worlds. A headline from *ZDnet* of this period had read, "Smartphone applications represent the new land rush for mobile technology vendors and the new gold rush for software developers." In my Entrepreneurship 101 class with Professor Chuck Sacco—a technology entrepreneur and start-up adviser in his own right—everyone was hungry, ravenous even, to develop and launch the next blockbuster app.

Later to become the assistant dean of Drexel's Charles D. Close School of Entrepreneurship and director of Drexel's Baiada Institute for Entrepreneurship, Professor Sacco was known as a Renaissance man. (He was versed in all kinds of business, cultural, and athletic pursuits and literally enjoyed going to Renaissance fairs with his family.) His motto was "Be valuable by being versatile."

Chuck Sacco had founded a few tech companies, one of which had been PhindMe, an app he cofounded and led that connected businesses to customers on their mobile devices. Later he sold it to Movitas LLC, a provider of mobile technology solutions to the travel and tourism industries.

As an educator, Professor Sacco was not a lead-you-by-the-hand kind of teacher but more of a guide who empowered you. His approach was to give you the tools and fundamentals for your growth, while cultivating an environment conducive to the flourishing of your own entrepreneurial ideas. Whatever advice, input, help, or encouragement you needed from then on, he was there. For me, that was optimal.

In his business circles, Professor Sacco was known for being strategic—a quality I admired—and as someone who kept his cards close to his chest. In an interview for one of Drexel's communications newsletters from those years, he was asked what drove him. The follow-up question was whether he was naturally competitive. Professor Sacco said he was competitive and that

> winning is good. But I think it's ultimately about doing a good job. Getting something built. At the end of the day, if you're focusing on winning and not focusing on adding value, I think maybe you're not doing the right thing. You can win sometimes and be a real jerk and not be doing the right thing. I'd rather be slightly less successful and have done good. Have really made a difference. Created something that people use, that they like, that they want.

Without knowing it at the time, I'm sure that his philosophy about adding value and making a difference in people's lives had an influence on the direction I took toward social entrepreneurship. It also laid the groundwork for my own conclusion that product is king.

Professor Sacco recognized my ambition and encouraged me not to be afraid to think and act boldly. At the same time, he also helped me recognize my weaknesses—starting with my tendency to be impulsive. When you're confident, the ability to act decisively, without hesitation, can be a superpower. However, it is a double-edged sword when it comes to taking risks. Being impulsive in making important decisions can derail your efforts before you can correct course.

Professor Sacco helped me find a balance. Before taking action on any great idea or potential partnership or opportunity, I learned from him to *try* to slow down and take my time to deliberate. Timing really is everything. I would see this over and over—that it's not so much *what* you do but *when* you do it. You can make the absolute right decision but at the wrong time. However you dice it, a right decision at the wrong time is still going to be a wrong decision.

Later on, at my own company my team members would hold their collective breath whenever I'd float a major decision and send everyone into action. It would come across as impulsive or as a big roll of the dice. Not so. Thanks to lessons learned from Professor Sacco, I could still use my assets of street hustle and grit, but before sending the troops into battle I would have thought through as many contingencies as possible.

Merging what I had learned from hood wisdom with my actual university business studies was empowering. From a competitive standpoint, the two perspectives gave me an edge and became the most exciting part of my first two years at Drexel. The fact is that I was impatient and hungry to get in on the tech boom. Again, I'm grateful to have been slowed down enough to make sure that I had some skills and real-world knowledge before diving in.

Where I was lacking was in hands-on work experience for an established business or in a corporate or organizational structure. That had been the plan all along, and one of the reasons that I'd chosen Drexel—because it offered a co-op year that would let me gain workplace skills and experience in earning money in the business world. My plan for the future was still to stick it out and get an MBA, then climb the ladder in the field of finance—maybe in New York in some kind of mergers and acquisitions—before later starting my own company.

A great plan? Absolutely. But a funny thing happened on the way to that destination. You've heard some of that story already, but some of it you haven't heard. Just to give you a preview, I hope you can relate to those twists and turns and ups and downs when the conventional path does not take you where it's supposed to at all.

Yet one more reason for not following a path.

My third year in Philadelphia was a roller coaster.

My six-month co-op at Fannie Mae—the government-backed mortgage lending institution for lower- to middle-income families—ought to have been a great fit for my interest in working in a for-profit arena but with a focus on helping struggling families become homeowners. The irony, as I thought about it later, was that the whole financial meltdown that had sent my family into deep poverty and functional homelessness had come about in part because of unethical lending practices that arose during the housing boom of the mid-2000s. Lenders gave money to borrowers with poor credit, and when the housing bubble burst in 2007, those homeowners couldn't pay their mortgages and defaulted—sending the banks and financial institutions into what was called the "subprime meltdown." Fannie Mae received a lot of the blame, although it was really the fault of the financial institutions that sought insurance for loans for applicants who shouldn't have been insured. Still, there was blame enough to go around. Everyone was just high on the fumes of the boom.

Call that a cautionary tale for all. Booms go bust, always, and there's a lot of fool's gold in the rushes that create economic bubbles. Of course, we know that bubbles can't last forever. One of the lessons I tried to extract from looking at what created the meltdown was a clearer understanding of the predatory loan mentality. At the time, I wasn't exploring that issue as closely as I would later, but it had important implications—not just for toxic mortgage and payday loans but for loans to students trying to pay for college and even for entrepreneurs looking for venture capital. My Big Ma would have stated it plainly: *If it seems too good to be true, it is.*

The bailout in the last part of 2008, fortunately, had kept Fannie Mae from being shut down. The agency was put it into conservatorship, and over the next year Congress repaired the regulations enough to get it back up and running securely again.

By the time I arrived for my internship in 2012, there were new and stricter financial rules in place, and overall the organization was being run ethically and efficiently. That was the good news for me. The bad news was that I found my immediate supervisor to be an extremely difficult boss who was ineffective, unfocused, and, in my view at least, allowed an unprofessional, and at times racist, work environment to exist. There were a number of smaller issues that I saw in need of addressing, but whenever I tried to offer to help, I was roundly dismissed.

For the first and only time in my life, I came close to being fired. Instead, I made good use of our branch office's Human Resources Department and then went to my supervisor directly and explained my complaints, which proactively discouraged any form of retaliation. The lesson was twofold. First, I realized that I was not fit to work for anyone but myself. Apparently, I had problems with authority. If people were using their personal lives to justify being uncivil, I for sure would say something about it. This new reality threw my original career plan to go to work for a corporation or large institution out the window. Now I had to rely on my entrepreneurial chops for my next moves.

Second, I was not comfortable with the old-school system of making interns, assistants, and other employees feel they couldn't contribute ideas and suggestions for helping run the business more effectively or profitably. I told myself: *Years from now, when I hire people to work for me, they will always have a voice.*

Little did I know that "years from now" would turn into less than a year later!

I should point out that my co-op experience was extreme. Before I left home, I'd worked at the library and at other part-time jobs, and I'm thankful for that exposure to how different work settings operate. But just in case you decide you too aren't fit for working for someone else and you want to walk out on your day job that's not your dream but that pays the bills, be prepared for the next big lesson I had to learn after deciding to be my own boss: *sacrifice*.

In 2012–2013 (and even today), "wantrepreneur" was a term we started to hear a lot that went along with the whole gold rush mentality. Everybody started to call themselves an "entrepreneur." Most of them just wanted to have the trappings of success, not all of the sacrifice, sweat, toil, and risk entailed in conceiving, creating, launching, and running a company. Everyone and their puppy (all right, I love puppies) wanted to be the next Mark Zuckerberg and cofound a start-up in their dorm room (as he did with Facebook in his sophomore year at Harvard) and then drop out of college to run it and become a multi-multi-billionaire. In 2013, Facebook was nine years old and Zuckerberg was worth something like $25 billion.

To a degree, you could understand the wantrepreneurs who had the desire to create the next hot app, achieve some traction, and then sell it for a few hundred million dollars. Nothing wrong with that. The part that was little understood was that you didn't just launch and then watch it zoom out to the stratosphere like a rocket ship. I'd hear peers talking about wanting to start a company and I'd ask if they were willing to deal with all the ups and downs and daily stresses, and they'd say, "Oh, no, I'm going to sell it and move on."

This kind of conversation was not relegated to this period, in fact. Down the road, I'd ask the same questions of would-be entrepreneurs coming to me for advice: Were they willing to sleep on people's couches and take huge risks with investors' money and maybe choose to give up their salary to afford the things it takes to keep a company afloat? Not knowing the terrain, they'd be surprised by this question. But once you study the lay of the land, you realize that trying to support yourself off the beaten track is a form of speculation and really not for everyone.

Part of making your choice is about adjusting your values. If your aim is mainly to acquire success and money, there are dependable paths that can lead to those goals. If your aim is to develop a product, service, or unique content that adds value to people's lives, and if you are also excited to learn and grow, sacrifice, and do the hard work required for success to happen, then you won't be disappointed as you carve out your own path. But patience and stamina are required.

There's another myth circulating, a Cinderella story about so-called accidental entrepreneurs who strike it rich with their first attempt at building an idea into a business. In fact, most of the iconic tech successes came after that entrepreneur had made earlier attempts—some that failed and some that were modestly successful. Mark Zuckerberg is a case in point of someone who had been tinkering with tech ideas for a while. He had proven himself enough that when he needed capital, his family and the connections made through them were available and helpful.

Sophia Amoruso, founder of Nasty Gal, the e-commerce women's fashion and accessory company that she started in 2006 as a side hustle among many, had taken off meteorically. A literal rags-to-riches story, Nasty Gal's rise was fueled in part by the recession and also by a desire for distinctive clothing at lower prices. Revenues would later put Sophia's net worth, at age thirty-two, at an estimated $280 million, and in June 2016 *Forbes* magazine named her one of the "richest self-made women" in America.

What none of the wantrepreneurs in my circle knew

back in the day at Drexel was that later on, in November 2016, five months after Sophia's debut on the *Forbes* list, Nasty Girl filed for bankruptcy (en route to a demolition-style restructuring before being put into new hands)—one of the more spectacular and highly publicized entrepreneurial failures of recent years. As time would tell, Sophia would rebound with a different brand identity based on her book *#Girlboss* and use her platform to achieve success as a global media entrepreneur and influencer, using her message of resilience to spark a women's #girlboss movement.

One moral of the story would be a reminder that failure doesn't have to be a dead end. There would be other take-aways, including the perils of spending too much money on marketing and advertising and not putting enough resources toward making sure the product is treated as king. One of Nasty Gal's big mistakes would be identified as not having done enough to cultivate repeat business. (I'll talk more later about how I had to learn that lesson.) Also, when a founder steals more thunder than the product itself, you're looking at a Cinderella story that can come to an end when the clock strikes midnight and there is no one around to wave a magic wand.

Some of these events hadn't played out yet when I was looking around at all of the wantrepreneurs and observing this gold rush mentality. Green as I was, I definitely wanted to differentiate myself and be seen as serious—not only as a student of entrepreneurship but as someone with skills and commitment to the long haul. When contemplating what might be my calling card, I tried to draw from everything that I'd been learning and researching as to the kind of product or app I'd want to create.

If there had been one theme to the steady stream of ideas keeping me awake at night, the heading above all of them would have been the concept of *access*. With Tweens and Teens Entertainment, Inc., the theme was access to organized, affordable (free) fun for the youth of Birmingham— something that hadn't existed before. In high school, my nonprofit had provided access to volunteer hours at prominent charities for those of us who had been shut off from volunteer opportunities. Even at my not so successful co-op experience, I still learned about the importance of creating access to government-backed loans for middle- and lower-income home buyers.

My hunch is that many of us have themes that come up for us a lot, themes that reflect and reveal our values and priorities. As you navigate your life's direction, I think it can be helpful to look within to find out what those themes might be.

Again, whether you're trying to write a college essay, come up with a business idea, strategy, or start-up mission, or solve a pressing societal concern, you have much to learn from looking at your important themes. Before you even land on the answer or the idea you're trying to develop, start to pay attention to the questions you've asked yourself over the years.

Trust me, your answer comes almost magically when you figure out the question.

Once I came to the conclusion that I wasn't going to go the traditional big corporate executive route, I felt so *relieved*. That would have been the easier path, when you think about it, but it just wasn't me. Now I was free to be who I was and to stake out my own claim. A riskier path, yes, but it was also liberating.

Just as 2013 got under way, at the age of twenty-one, I could feel the ground shifting and my trajectory changing. The pace of everything I was learning and doing seemed to accelerate. The future was still uncertain, but at this particular inflection point I suddenly felt ready to try my hand at actual entrepreneurship.

How? That was the question. Or should I say—*What?*

A couple of strokes of phenomenal timing helped me answer that question. The first, now that I was in the second semester of my co-op year, was the requirement as part of the program at Drexel's Close School of Entrepreneurship that I start an actual company. The other well-timed blessing was that earlier in the academic year (while I was still at Fannie Mae), I was invited to take part in another internship, of sorts, that was housed at both Drexel and at Penn. Dorm Room Fund, as it was called, was a venture capital initiative that was overseen by eleven student entrepreneurs who mentored, ran, and funded the tech start-ups of fellow student entrepreneurs. The first time I attended a skull session at Penn to discuss the goals of Dorm Room Fund and met some of the other participants, I felt an intellectual, energy-infused chemistry with practically everyone involved. There was a like-mindedness that allowed us to communicate and collaborate at an incredible level. These were my people.

Most of the participants became friends for life. Later, when I wanted to start a company, my first hires came from this group.

Dorm Room Fund was the brainchild of Josh Kopelman, an entrepreneur who had launched his own start-up in his dorm room—as an undergrad at Penn's Wharton School of business. Before graduating, he ran the company, grew his business, and later went public with it. That told me right there that you didn't have to drop out to get your start in the tech world.

After graduation, Josh launched another company, built it and sold it even more dramatically, running it for a while before making his exit (the Tech American Dream). And then—because three is always a good number—he created yet another start-up. That one he sold as fast as you can ask, *What next?* He answered the question by going to the investment side of things and becoming one of the leading venture capitalists in the world.

Josh could have transplanted his operations to Silicon Valley or to any of the other tech hubs, but he believed that Philly was rich with underdeveloped, true entrepreneurial talent in the technology space. So after establishing his firm, First Round Capital, he may have seen Dorm Room Fund and the $500,000 he used to seed it as one means of putting back into the soil that had enriched him. That is an example of the attitude that motivates social entrepreneurs, who tend to ask themselves, *How can my success feed the successes of others?* In fact, when Josh and his wife opened the doors to their nonprofit foundation, they went further and provided funding specifically for social entrepreneurs.

On First Round Capital's website, Josh, a nonconformist in his own way, wrote an untraditionally personal mission statement that talked about his college days at Wharton. He recalled:

While others were cramming for tests at all hours of the night, I decided to co-found a company called Infonautics Corporation and was fortunate to take it public on the NASDAQ in 1996. I then had this crazy idea to allow anyone to buy and sell used books, music and DVDs online and launched Half.com in July of 1999. The timing worked out and we were acquired by eBay in July of 2000. I followed Half.com with one more company called Turntide that Symantec quickly acquired.

The price eBay paid Josh Kopelman for Half.com was $374 million. While other dot-com businesses of the late 1990s spent tons of money on marketing, Josh and his team had come up with a genius idea to create brand awareness. They bought a town. Or should I say, they rebranded a town. For very little money compared to what other companies were spending on advertising and brand awareness schemes, they paid Halfway, Oregon, to change its name to Half.com. That literally put their brand on the map, and once consumers got to know the product, which was simple and easy to use, the brand swiftly took the e-commerce world by storm. When he sold Half.com to eBay, Josh was twenty-eight years old—only seven years out of college.

Following the same principle for developing a top-shelf product, he won praise even more swiftly for the anti-spam technology Turntide, which was declared "magic" by reviewers. For a cool $28 million, Symantec scooped up Turntide within six months after it hit the market. Once Josh Kopelman segued from being an owner, inventor, and entrepreneur to becoming an investor and venture capitalist, he was seen right away as having a Midas touch. First Round Capital played a pivotal role in providing early, meaningful money and other support for such brands as Uber, LinkedIn, and Blue Apron—to name only a few.

At Dorm Room Fund, I was fortunate enough to observe and get to know Josh Kopelman and to see the kinds of ideas that were compelling to him, how he scrutinized a start-up's potential value, and how he harnessed his high energy. From then on, I regarded him as one of my most important mentors and role models. Even though we came from different backgrounds (he's Jewish from an upper-middle-class, highly educated Long Island family), I always felt Josh understood the plight of minorities and marginalized communities.

When you have a mentor who is up on a pedestal, that changes the dynamic. But I could relate to Josh; I'd even say we had certain similar styles and approaches to decision-making. Like me, he could be intense and impulsive, with maybe, like me, some impatience or even a short attention span thrown in. He embodied a readiness to take strong positions on opportunities, something I very much wanted to do as well. At the same time, Josh could be completely matter-of-fact and was always cool under fire. Those were qualities I sought to develop too.

Best of all, for me, Josh Kopelman loved generating positive action. He naturally looked for upsides, even in downturns. When asked about why he wasn't more concerned in those periods as booms were going bust, Josh would say, as he told *Fortune* magazine, "Having weathered the dot com crash and the 2007–2008 Great Recession, I know that great companies are built in all types of markets and continue searching for amazing founders building incredible businesses."

To which I would add, incredible businesses rest on the foundations of incredible products.

You could never predict how Josh was going to react to a pitch at Dorm Room Fund, partly because he wanted to hear from all of us first about how we felt. As the website for First Round Capital puts it, he prefers to stay open, rather than be associated with one investment sector over another: "Instead of predicting the future, we look to our founders to convince us of what's next. . . . The one thing each of our companies has in common—we met when they were a couple of people with an idea and a slide deck."

Nothing else could have offered me the education that Dorm Room Fund did when I found myself ready to develop my own projects. After all, I'd been given the chance to sit on the side of the investor. We heard from hundreds of companies. When I witnessed what worked, as far as presentations went, I learned from that. Plus, when I heard about the choices others had made, either in their pitch or in the steps they took to develop their companies, those lessons taught me how to avoid their mistakes. Getting a chance to evaluate whether you should invest in a business or product certainly helps to inform you as to where you should put your resources to make you and your idea appealing to investors and VCs.

We'd see an interesting idea from someone who hadn't

done any market research about the possibility of impact. We'd hear from a founder who gave a fine presentation but didn't really get the product, didn't have any domain expertise, or had a flawed business model. One of my pet peeves was listening to a bunch of MBAs who had not built any kind of model but who were trying to sell their product based on their own prestige and brand.

Sometimes we would see a product that was such a great idea but the pitch was off. In those instances, we would work with that entrepreneur and help them to get their presentation up to speed. We could then wholeheartedly recommend giving them money.

The best pitches were those from founders who were passionate, who offered well-developed products, who had the ingenuity to show the need for their product, and who knew their stuff, enough to get all of us excited. That's when we would all know this was going to be a great business.

Passion, passion, passion.

You can't say it enough times. It's contagious. You can't fake it either. That's why the product must be king. Fall in love with what you are selling and you aren't even selling.

You're probably thinking that's exactly what happened when I struck upon my idea for an app to help students access all that money in unclaimed scholarships. Well, almost. As it actually happened, during the couple months or so leading up to that Call to Action moment, I had begun to develop an app idea inspired by everything I'd learned from Dorm Room Fund.

This was a no-brainer as far as I was concerned. In truth, I wanted to start small, on the niche side of things, emphasizing technology and maybe coming up with a proprietary algorithm. My strategy, borrowing from others, was to get my name out there and then follow up with something that could go out to the mainstream. My first run was to build a start-up based on a concept that I called Ventunary—a merger of the words "venture" and "dictionary."

Access for those without it, as usual, was my concern. The concept was to offer an app that matched emerging entrepreneurs and their ideas with sources of investment and venture capital. At this point in time, I hadn't yet been in a position to go knock on Silicon Valley doors, but it seemed to me that Ventunary would make a world of difference for innovative content creators without connections.

I'd even gone so far as to partner with a cofounder, Elijah, also a student at Drexel, who was brilliant at what he did, coming up with logos, design, and other proprietary elements. He might not have been as convinced as I was that Ventunary was going to hit us a home run, but I tried to remind myself that not everyone was going to share the same enthusiasm for something that only existed in theory. There was a lot of legwork and research to do to build a database that was going to impress potential investors. That fell to me to do, since it was my original concept and I knew what I was looking for.

At a certain point, I began to feel that Elijah and I weren't complementary as collaborators for the long run. In time, I'd learn a great deal more about finding partners in my ventures who are not only like-minded but who also have different skillsets that balance mine out. Super-creative, Elijah was someone you'd want helping you develop important details of a product—a logo, a look, a signature. As far as wanting to oversee the day-to-day responsibilities of running a start-up while still in college, however, I didn't see that as his thing. We sort of parted ways, not bitterly, although I found it uncomfortable.

The lasting lesson was to not be in a hurry to partner. We worked out something that he would still get once Ventunary was profitable, and that too was a lesson—make sure to put verbal agreements in writing, even if you only write up a brief deal memo for yourselves to follow.

My memory of this time is that it was almost a rerun of all those months I spent researching scholarships back in high school. Only now I was working into the early hours of the morning at the computer lab, trying to stay up to date on classwork, doing some scholarship and college admissions help for friends, and pushing hard on Ventunary—researching endless pathways with creative keywords, building a database, and tinkering with criteria for the technology that would match investors and aspiring entrepreneurs. I'd learned enough about coding that I could loosely develop a demo, although only enough to show on a slide deck. We would need a real techie to build a patented matching system.

Right as the winter nights started to subside and warmer weather kicked in, I was working late one night when one of the professors stopped by and greeted me. She was also regularly in her office late, and on occasion we'd walk out together.

"You're really on to something, aren't you?" she asked with a smile.

I shrugged, telling her, "I hope so." Honestly, I wasn't sure this was the product I could develop as king.

She predicted, "Whether it's this or something else, as hard as you're working, I know you're going to do great things."

Her words were the reassurance that I needed just then, and they came back to me not many nights later when I got mad enough about the inequities of paying for college to conceive of the big idea that had been lurking in the back of my mind.

The minute the solution for this urgent question arrived in my brain, there was no question about what I needed to do next. By the time I arrived at home in my actual dorm room and started to review the database of scholarships that I'd made already, I realized that I had most of the research done.

The name had come to me right away from having heard athletes talk about their athletic scholarships as getting their "scholly." The vibe was cool, young, and appealing to high school, college, and graduate school students. All I needed now was someone to help me with a dope logo and web design, at least to start looking for investors. Then I could bring in tech partners who knew how to design apps.

There was no one in my mind who could design a look better than Elijah. He was tech-savvy, smart, and fast. This meant I had to swallow my pride and go see if he would consider working with me on it. Instead of offering equity, I decided to pay him for his work. Ironically, I had recently gotten a reimbursement from one of my scholarship funds for some expenses and could draw from that to pay for help in designing an app that would help more people access scholarship money. There was that theme again.

When I caught up with Elijah in an empty classroom where we took a course together, I asked if he had a minute to talk.

"Sure . . ." He shrugged, not instantly receptive. Then I described my vision and showed him my concept for matching criteria. "So basically," I said, "what took me over seven months of grueling work to find scholarships that were a fit for me, will be an almost instantaneous match for applicants." He loved it. He could see the social relevance of the effort, and he approved.

"What are you thinking about?" he asked, wanting me

to name the price I was willing to pay. Instead, I asked him to name his price. Hey, I learned some of that from my mother, who was excellent at being frugal in negotiation and making the other person feel like they got what they wanted.

Elijah asked for $2,000. For a college start-up with no guarantees of traction, it was a lot. In less than a month, he came back with the work that might have cost me $50,000 or more in the competitive tech and design worlds. Elijah knew that, and he not only allowed me to be able to afford his help but did a fantastic job. He used so many elements that I loved: a cherry red color on white and vice versa, a puppy in a graduation cap sniffing the ground—i.e., looking for scholarships—and a super-simple, clean look for the app. It was everything I wanted and more.

My next step was to bring in two cofounders who would build out the technology of the app. Bryson Alef, a fellow recipient of the Coca-Cola Foundation scholarship, was a razor-sharp, detail-oriented friend I'd first met when we were flown to Atlanta for a gathering of all the scholarship recipients. Bryson attended Amherst and had been developing apps on his own already. My other cofounder, Nicholas Pirollo, was a fellow student at Drexel who was also a tech wiz and a natural leader, as well as an entrepreneur who came from the school of "make things happen."

When I presented them with the template I'd developed for users—a list of questions asking for state of residence, whether interested in scholarships based on need, merit, or both, GPA, academics and extracurriculars, and so on—they went to work to develop a matching system with scholarships that would give us the biggest, fastest bang for our buck. They came back with something faster and more dramatic than I could have dreamed of. In minutes, an applicant could fill out their profile, then click Done, and a list of possible scholarships would appear—20,000 possible sources of money for college. We tested it, worked out a few glitches, and then, in early April 2013, Nick and I met in the computer lab, where I'd been more or less living, and took a look at the Scholly app on our phones.

This time when I tested it and looked down at the thousands of scholarships now at my fingertips, there were tears in my eyes. We had made it happen.

This had to be the closest thing to giving birth that I had ever experienced.

This product was king. It was going to make a difference in people's lives *and* make us some money. This was a dream come true.

There was so much more to do, so much more work to come to get investments and users. Resolved to pace myself, I knew that realistically, even if we got some venture capital so we could start marketing, there was little likelihood that we would see a profit right away.

Great news, though: thanks to how I'd learned to use resources growing up, everything was about to go into warp speed. In the craziest of all scenarios, I would soon be known as a superhero in Philly—for reasons I could never have predicted.

If there is one takeaway from this time that I can underscore for you, it's my belief that for all of us there are opportunities and mentors that show up all the time. It's our job to look for them, notice them, appreciate them, and soak up every bit of knowledge that we can from them.

If you haven't noticed them, you might be wondering where your mentors and opportunities have been. Maybe that's a sign that you've been playing it too safe, that you're sticking to the beaten path. Once you diverge from it, mentors and opportunities do start to show up. Once they do, and once they have helped you grow, be prepared to put all that knowledge to use.

Here's where the competition does start to get tough, so lean into the challenges and put your resources to the test. If you don't, somebody else will.

Chapter 7

The Legend of the Big Break

LESSONS IN SWIMMING WITH THE SHARKS

Are we gladiators or are we bitches?

—Harrison Wright (Columbus Short), second in
command to Olivia Pope (Kerry Washington), *Scandal*
(created by Shonda Rhimes), season 3, episode 1

In case I haven't said it enough, under any and all circumstances whenever you decide to become the creator of your own destiny, you require serious daring and you deserve tremendous praise. When you make up your mind that you are going to be the first person in your family to attend college, your determination takes independence and audacity. When you decide you are going to leave a secure job that feels like it's not taking you anywhere and do something that's tougher yet a path that allows you to learn and grow, you are acting as an entrepreneur of your own life.

When you decide to reinvent yourself at an age when

others have decided to coast downhill (because it takes less effort), you have said the ultimate YES to yourself when the world is telling you NO. In my view, when you refuse to let uncertainty keep you from solving problems that affect others and you believe you can make a difference in your own bottom line and that of others, that makes you a gladiator!

Practically speaking, the choice to go in a different direction from most people you know, to carve out your own lane and then to push yourself to a higher calling, is along the same lines as choosing to "level up." Whoever coined that term probably played a video game or two, most of which typically depict your advancement in the game as moving up to the next level. You've already earned your points, badges, and coins, and now you're going to face challenges and foes you've never encountered before.

When you choose to *level up*, you may feel you have something to prove—and you do! Consider yourself an upperclassman/woman at what you do. You may have to learn all those lessons of hustle, grit, scholarship, and faith again, only now at the advanced level. Just know, by the way, that there is nothing wrong with asking what others who leveled up did to avoid the pitfalls and combat the competition.

Remember, gladiators train before they go fight the lions at the Colosseum.

My take on this process comes from the period when

my unpaved path required me to level up quickly. Not only was I attempting to become a CEO of my own company, but I was learning to collaborate with my cofounders to actually build the app together and begin to beta test it to quietly attract users. Plus, I was in the midst of juggling two majors, hoping to graduate on time and to continue to do well in my classes.

For the first time in my life I had to learn the age-old lesson that I'd missed before: *you can't always do it all.* Not when you're deciding to level up and focus on something you've never attempted before. With that in mind, I dropped my finance major and focused instead on graduating with just my entrepreneurship degree. That decision saved me. Even then, when graduation rolled around in the spring of 2015, I still had two classes that I had to finish up after the day of ceremonies.

At the time, whenever I looked at the examples of other start-ups that went rapidly from incubation to the hottest, most profitable brands, the stories that captured my interest always included a chapter on how those companies got their big break. Most of them involved an angel with first-round money or a pitch over drinks that led to a VC deciding to preempt all other interest with a major influx of money; those deals sometimes prohibited other investors from making offers and also made looking for other investments unnecessary. The more I looked into those stories, though, the more I saw that the legend of the big break was not always grounded in reality. True, there are anecdotes of founders being given huge opportunities that they could easily have blown, but didn't. Yet in such cases, what you learn is that those founders had leveled up after a series of smaller breaks that led to the bigger breaks.

In Hollywood, the legend of the big break is equally prevalent. Veterans of the entertainment industry will tell you that there is no such thing as overnight success. Usually, before that big role that sends an actor into orbit, there were smaller roles and years of taking classes and sleeping on people's couches. By the same token, when the defining role finally happened, yes, that was a huge opportunity not to be missed. Such was the case for Jesse Williams, who seemed to burst on the scene in 2009 with his leading role as Dr. Jackson Avery on *Grey's Anatomy*. A graduate of Temple University in Philadelphia, where he had studied acting, theater, and film, Jesse initially had not sought a career in show business but instead became a public high school teacher, following in his parents' footsteps. In 2006, not long after moving to New York City, where he worked for a short time in a law firm, he made his theatrical debut at the Cherry Lane Theater to much acclaim. Stage roles soon led to his landing a little break with a small part on *Law and Order*. Over the next three years he was grinding, on the stage and in television and film, booking enough work to gain the experience and the exposure to be ready when the opportunity to audition for *Grey's Anatomy* arrived.

Jesse's ability to bring insights to his craft from his experience as a teacher and in law has made him more competitive, more versatile, and more influential in the long run—not only as an actor but as a director, entrepreneur, spokesperson, and activist.

With the explosion of multiple channels that make up the universe of social media, of course, we have a whole new category of internet celebrities and influencers hoping to achieve their big break. Maybe now more than ever—especially at a time when the COVID-19 pandemic has required shutdowns and social distancing—there is a hunger for true tales of overnight sensations. Some of these stories don't sound so far-fetched when content suddenly "goes viral" (although that's an expression that has lost its luster in the time of the deadly novel coronavirus).

In reality, most of the internet celebrities with a rags-to-riches story rarely hit on their first appearances, despite their reputation for coming out of nowhere. Those who do gain traction and staying power usually had earlier followings that grew them a considerable number of views and followers incrementally over time.

Bottom line—you've taken a path that doesn't exist, so take advantage of every break you can get. The little breaks make the big breaks possible. Just be prepared when you level up to "swim with the sharks," as they say.

In my case, that metaphor was right on point.

One lesson that I most hope to share from my efforts to launch a social enterprise with no capital is that what you lack may be exactly the thing that gets you what you need. *All that glitters is not gold* would be a running theme for me in the formative years of Scholly. It applies to all of us.

More credit is due to my mother and to my Big Ma for teaching me not to be intimidated or outdone because others have resources that I don't. Momma would get me to think differently, asking me, "Well, what do you have that they don't?"

Whenever I was about to bang my head against a wall because we didn't have a marketing or PR budget, I'd think of Momma's question and remember that I had the ability to hustle up my own marketing and PR. Leveling up is all about finding a way out of no way.

For every start-up, there are several critical factors, including a great product (for an app, that means starting with a well-developed and well-run beta test that lets you get all the bugs out of the system) and a business model that is simple and affordable but also profitable. You also need a solid, realistic business plan so that investors can see you aren't going to be reckless if they're willing to write you a check. Without some means of creating exposure, however, there is very little you can do to build a solid platform that can sustain your business.

PR is an essential—whether you budget for it or try to put together your own press materials and develop your own media contacts. Recently, I spoke to this point as a member of a multigenerational panel on marketing for tech companies. It was interesting to hear how the generations seemed to feel differently about how effective do-it-yourself public relations and marketing can be. The under-thirty founders—Millennials and Gen Next/Gen Z-ers—easily understood the value of becoming known in smaller, local, and niche markets. Baby Boomer and Gen X entrepreneurs didn't see the point of pursuing local news, college publications or radio shows, social media posts, and random websites. The old-school Madison Avenue mentality still seems to be to go big or go home.

My point on the panel was to say that if you need exposure, why not be willing to start small? You'll be amazed at how hungry all kinds of local outlets are for content to fill space—newspapers, church bulletins, business bloggers, producers of radio shows and podcasts, you name it. Once you get a few pieces of media to show for yourself, you kick off a domino effect.

In our discussion that day a question came up that we've all heard frequently: What really is the difference between public relations and marketing campaigns? I'm always happy when someone's willing to ask it because, until you've run a business, the lines tend to be blurred. The simplest explanation is that public relations focuses on building brand awareness, while marketing is directly connected to making sales. Some people call PR "free advertising." Broadly, PR provides a means of gaining publicity and promotion for your brand (or you) from press and other media outlets. Marketing may include some of that effort, but it's more a plan of action that allows you to identify your market, how and where to reach your buyers, and how you're going to promote and sell your product, content, or service to those consumers. Advertising (commercials, digital ads, print, radio, and TV ads, and so on) is often critical to sales and is also part of your overall marketing strategy. Running ads for your business can sometimes ring up a pricey tab, whereas getting exposure through public relations shouldn't cost you a dime—other than for the PR people you hire.

And again, without capital, sometimes the PR help you hire is *you*. Without the financial resources needed for creating early exposure, I had to be imaginative, so I went back to the lessons of hustle and charm. After I spent hours trying to come up with a halfway decent press release, it occurred to me that Drexel's award-winning Department of Communication offered degrees with specialization in PR and marketing and more. It couldn't hurt, I thought, to see if maybe some of the motivated communication students, including some of those who worked on the college magazine and newspaper, could be convinced to help me get some press for Scholly. Even though at the time—April 2013—we were still officially in incubation and not even operational yet, I wanted to start creating some local buzz. My attitude was that whatever exposure Scholly got would be reflected positively back on the department and on Drexel.

When I arrived at the main offices of the Department of Communications to give an impromptu pitch, I naturally started with my own story, told from my heart, authentically, and waited to hear from them how best to mine it for publicity. By the time I was done they were all revved up, and the main editor was adamant that "everyone in Philadelphia needs to hear about this app!" A staff writer added, "Everyone in the country needs to hear about the app."

They believed in Scholly so much, and were such champions of my story and my purpose, that they offered not only to help me with press materials but also to make phone calls to media outlets on my behalf. Then they asked if it would be okay to run a story on us, suggesting that they could help get us an initial round of users. Now we were marketing—hitting publicity and sales.

In a moment of kismet, someone in the PR department had the fantastic idea to pitch me to appear on a local TV news show, Fox 29 in Philly. It so happened that the station was hosting an on-air fundraiser for college financial aid to low-income students. During a couple of pledge breaks, I had a chance to give a demo of the app *on camera* and show off how easy and fast it was. I demonstrated filling out the profile, answering the eight questions, pressing a button, and then seeing a list of several hundred scholarships pop up that you could apply for. A feature I was excited to promote was an option to check merit *or* financial need, so as to reassure our pool of potential consumers that every income level could find scholarships. The other aspect to the process I wanted to emphasize was the availability of scholarships for already enrolled students and grad students, not just for incoming freshmen.

Within minutes of our appearance, the TV station was deluged with requests as to how to get our app. We hadn't even gone live with the app yet. In haste, my cofounders and I settled on a business model that would offer onetime downloads for 99 cents. Still technically in beta testing, we imagined that the cost would go up, but that this would work for inaugural users. In hindsight, that was a rookie mistake and not reflective of the value we felt the app held for our users. However, the minute we quietly put the word out, we turned around and overnight had 10,000 users!

This was not our big break by any means, but on a local basis, wow, Philadelphia was paying attention. The Drexel communications team did a feature touting the excitement generated by my appearance on Fox 29. That's the magic of getting that first PR piece—it becomes a promotional tool for more pieces.

In August 2013, thanks again to the communications department, I was invited to attend a press gathering about making college more affordable. I knew that reporters from *USA Today* would be in attendance, and at the opportune moment I hustled over and introduced myself, offering the two-minute Scholly elevator pitch I'd honed by this point. Then I added, "If you'd want to do a possible feature, I'm available."

The way I said it, as if I might have to check my schedule, was hustle all the way, but they didn't mind. Sure enough, they called for an interview, and shortly after that, the *USA Today* piece showed up, as expected, even though I had no idea yet what the difference in impact would be between getting local press and appearing in a national piece. What I also didn't expect was that the story would be prominently featured on the digital homepage of the whole paper. This was such an out-of-body experience that my friends decided we had to celebrate, and they took me out for a drink! One of my first drinks ever. That's how huge the *USA Today* article was.

Still, I had no idea what was to come. Business cranked up and boomed.

The 99 cent onetime download fee made it appealing to everyone. In my gut, I knew that was going to be limiting down the road, but for now we were really living up to the social enterprise part of our mission. The more affordable the app was, the more accessible it was. The problem was that now we had to staff up and build infrastructure to make sure we were updating our database and servicing users—who were growing at the rate of 10,000 downloads a month.

Several more local papers and niche market magazines followed. Nick and Bryson reached out to their hometown and college contacts too, and the *USA Today* ripple became something of a smallish wave. This wasn't even heavy lifting for us.

In the fall, or what would officially be the start of my junior year, I walked by a stack of school publications and recognized a picture of myself on the cover of Drexel's *Market Street* magazine with a caption reading "True Life Superhero." Inside, the feature about Scholly had a cartoon version of me in a Superman outfit and cape, holding a fistful of dollars. I grabbed several copies in disbelief. They had not only interviewed me for the story but incorporated my childhood dreams into the illustrations. It was overwhelming—to the point of literally having to pinch myself.

Running a start-up became my full-time concern while my academic studies had to be addressed during the hours allotted for sleep. We were leveling up now. On our way to having 92,000 users, we lived and breathed Scholly, especially me. The crazy thing was that we were turning a profit from the word go and also changing the lives of our customers, who were starting to win scholarship awards.

As others have pointed out, learning to run a company while building it is a lot like building the airplane while flying it—not for the faint of heart. But by the spring of 2014, everything seemed to be running as smoothly as could be hoped.

That was when I got a call from Professor Sacco about an opportunity that he said could accelerate our growth. He may have mentioned that it could be a big break—or something along those lines. The feature in *USA Today*, it seemed, had brought Scholly to the attention of a couple of young producers who contacted Professor Sacco to see what he thought about the possibility of me coming on as a *Shark Tank* contestant. He recommended that I go for it, although there were risks to having that much exposure this early. We hadn't even incorporated yet.

I might have joked by saying, "Too much exposure? Too many users? Those would be wonderful problems to have."

Not thinking much would come of it, I said by all means to give them my info and then forgot all about it for the time being. Meanwhile, in early summer 2014, the big news for us was an online cover story being done on Scholly by BET.

When I told their editor about the shock of finding out that many millions of dollars in awards go unclaimed every year, they did some research and found out that approximately 1.5 million different scholarships are offered annually, totaling up to $3.4 billion in "free money." Even though I generally knew that, the numbers BET laid out were staggering. We could now proudly say that with our users we were earning $50,000 annually, thanks in part to block sales of downloads we were offering to school systems and institutions. In fact, with all of the great PR we'd been getting, the financial aid office at Drexel purchased blocks of download subscriptions for fellow students of mine.

In this same period, Scholly was chosen as one of *Inc.*'s sixteen "Coolest College Startups" of 2014. When they asked me to give them the brief pitch on the major issue we had solved as a start-up, this was my response:

The Pitch: "College is expensive, forcing students to take out thousands of dollars in student loans in order to foot the bill. As a result, many students are drowning in student debt. This has made many students and parents turn to scholarships and grants to pay for college education. The only problem with these scholarships, however, is that they are notoriously hard to find. Students are either forced to scour the Web or use websites that give them a list of thousands of scholarships they may not even qualify for."

The case for Scholly could not have been made more effectively, if I do say so myself. My same pitch was about to get a lot of play.

When I finally heard from the two young producers Professor Sacco had told me about, Michael Kramer and Allen Kirk, they seemed enthusiastic. But they let me know, in so many words, that Scholly might be a hard sell on their end. As far as I could tell in those days, the Sharks invested in entrepreneurs who developed and marketed physical products and only very infrequently in first-time CEOs of tech start-ups like mine.

The part that seemed compelling to them, apparently, was my personal story of overcoming the odds and earning $1.3 million in scholarships—what some would call my proof of concept. Michael and Allen promised to get back to me soon, but when I didn't hear right away, I sort of forgot about them all over again and went back to my daily grind.

On the way out of class one day that summer, my phone rang. It was Michael Kramer, telling me the main *Shark Tank* producers were fired up and wanted to "fast-track" my audition. Michael said, "That rarely happens. Almost never."

Most contestants take a lot longer to be vetted and have to weather more uncertainty. Now I started to get excited. The main *Shark Tank* producers wanted me to deliver an audition video to them at my earliest convenience.

With hustle as my guide, I immediately went into overdrive—tapping everyone I could at Drexel to help me produce the ultimate audition video.

Clearly, I come from the school of being willing to grind, of making things happen, and of finding a way to stand out. And as far as I was concerned, the video had to be *perfect*. For days before filming the audition video, I practiced my presentation over and over, until I could have recited it backwards. Once it was edited and audience-tested with as many friends as I could engage in the process, we sent it in to *Shark Tank*, hoping for the best.

What could have been months of waiting turned out to be a couple of weeks.

Producer Michael Kramer gave me the news: "We love what you have. We're flying you out here on the next-to-last day of shooting before hiatus."

Before I knew it, I was booked on a flight to Los Angeles, the land of palm trees and movie stars, and slated to show up at Sony Pictures studios at the crack of dawn on a Friday morning for my segment to film. The Little App that Could was about to climb its biggest mountain—in front of 10 million viewers!

Was this the Legend of the Big Break come true after all? Or was it too good to be true? Everything was moving as though it was all meant to be. When I finally met the two producers in person—who looked exactly the way you'd expect two high-energy, smart producers to look—I could tell they were almost as pumped as I was. However, they did warn all of us in the studio that morning that there was no guarantee we would shoot our segments that day. There was also no guarantee our segments would even air if they did get shot.

That didn't bother me. I had a good feeling. But then came the first real stumbling block in the whole *Shark Tank* saga so far, around midday. I was the last segment set to shoot, and they were already running behind schedule. The what-ifs started to eat away at my confidence. What if the Sharks were tired, hungry, or cranky? Until I walked through the doors to the set, they would have no idea who I was or what my business venture was. What if they'd maxed out their investments? What if another tech company had captured their interest and most of their bucks?

Chill, I told myself.

So I did. That is, until late in the afternoon when Michael and Allen came to the greenroom/holding area where I'd been waiting to go on.

Michael began, "Chris, listen, we've gone way over schedule and we just ran out of time. Sorry."

Was that *it*? I tried, not too successfully, to hide my disappointment.

Allen reassured me. "You have a couple of options. We're going to shoot some more segments tomorrow. If you can stay one more night, you can come back in the morning, and we'll try to get you up as one of the first to be seen. Or, if you have to fly back to Philly, we'll try to bring you back here in September."

If I waited until the fall, chances were good that our numbers would only get better and that might make Scholly more viable in front of the Sharks. On the other hand, I didn't like losing the momentum we'd gained.

Michael added another variable, admitting, "We can't promise to bring you back in September. We'd try to do that, but a lot can change over the summer."

"I'll stay and come back tomorrow morning," I said, going with my gut. I had no idea in that moment that at least one of the Sharks who would be the friendliest to me on our actual shoot was not on the panel that evening when they ran out of time. All I knew was that opportunities rarely come around twice. Even if this one wasn't unfolding exactly how I'd expected, my job was to *adapt* and have faith that it would work out as it was meant to be.

And so there I was the next morning, behind the double doors, a fish out of water taking a deep dive into the shark tank.

A true pressure cooker. When these moments happen for you—when a big, medium, or small break is on the line—hopefully you're ready to level up. If you remind yourself of your training and your readiness, that alone can help you calm your nerves and clear your mind.

In my case, I had put myself in Shark School to prepare for whatever they had to throw at me. Channeling my inner

Batman/Superman and Olivia Pope crisis management superstar all at once, I called on all the knowledge and information I'd studied in advance of any question they could possibly ask. I knew every answer like the back of my hand.

From the get-go, I'd been *on* it.

Scholarship came to my rescue. I'd watched almost every *Shark Tank* episode from all the previous seasons, learning from every candidate who had been on the show before, memorizing every challenge they'd been given and how they did or did not respond effectively. Thanks to experience I'd gained in the Dorm Room Fund and input from my mentors, Professor Chuck Sacco and Josh Kopelman, I'd mastered the language of negotiation. I could talk the talk. Without a doubt, I knew my business and had mastered my facts to where they were ready to fly off my tongue: revenue, the demographics of our users, detailed numbers related to valuation, projections, and marketing strategies.

An emphasis on financials was an often overlooked key to getting a good deal.

That had been a big piece of advice given to me by my producers: *Know those numbers inside and out.* They had been drilling me over the phone about them for weeks before my arrival in LA.

To this point, let me add that anytime you go into an interview or audition situation, do not skimp on doing your homework about the other person or people you are about to meet. It's always surprising to me when I call someone in for an interview and they haven't taken the time to learn everything they can about me, my company, or the type of business that we're in. With so much knowledge at our fingertips these days, there is actually no excuse other than laziness for showing up without making the effort. It's okay to ask your interviewers about themselves—mentioning, for example, that you've read something about a particular decision and you want to know more. That shows that you take initiative. Yes, the goal is to interview you, but people generally like to talk about themselves. If you can put your interviewer at ease, that helps you feel the same way.

There is always a power imbalance in every setting where you are going to be judged and are more or less at the mercy of the person on the other side of the desk—or, as we experience more and more these days, on the other side of the virtual meeting space. To address that imbalance, it can be so helpful to come with a feeling of confidence that you have something to offer that will be just as valuable to the person whose favor you hope to win.

That way, even if you walk away from an opportunity empty-handed from the exchange, you still have the integrity and value you had walking in.

Showing my sincerity and my knowledge, I believed, could certainly help me win favor with even the coldest of the Sharks. Not in a "I'm you're biggest fan" way but with humor and knowledge of their likes and dislikes.

The irony about to unfold was that, as prepared as I was to answer every question, they wouldn't get around to asking very many. That being said, I can tell you that the great gift of all that prep work was that instead of being intimidated by the Sharks, I stood there just before walking out onstage and felt admiration for how each of them had made their fortune as an entrepreneur.

Shark-taming lesson #1: *If you can get past your fear, you can learn a lot of what "they" know.*

This was the thought that kept running through my head as I waited for my cue. My strategy, by no means unusual, was to get them so excited that they would try to outbid each other for the opportunity to invest in my company.

Of course, all kinds of other scenarios could happen— as I was about to learn.

To make sense of what ended up happening, some more background may be in order. First, it may be common knowledge but it wasn't to me until I did some research and realized ahead of time that the bidding wars between the Sharks were sometimes exaggerated. The fireworks you see when you watch most reality shows on TV have more to do with show business than any real fight.

This show was no exception. I mean—who doesn't look forward to watching the Sharks get into a spat? The drama does get amplified, however, with the help of smoke and mirrors. There's a formula, a structure, that lends itself to the possibility of conflict. Still, the show's not scripted. When you first appear in front of the panel as an entrepreneur, the Sharks have no background on you or your business, and they have no plan as to how they might respond. Anything can happen. The point is, the more unpredictable the outcome, the more viewers the show can hook, right?

That much I knew going in. The best advice I'd been given, long before cameras rolled, was: *Be prepared for uncertainty.*

I waited to hear my name called, with that line as my mantra. As soon as the double doors began to glide open, I'd be stepping out onto the set—where I would stand under a blaze of white lights in front of a panel of five steely-eyed Sharks.

No matter how smoothly my pitch went, obviously there were variables I couldn't control. The five of them might all jump in at once, feud over who could make the best offer, and then all turn around and declare, "I'm *out!*" at the last minute. A lone Shark could show a lot of love but go way lower than the investment amount requested. That always posed a dilemma for the hopeful entrepreneur, who wouldn't want to leave with no offer at all. Or, as was sometimes the case, the Sharks could try to outbid one another, but then decide to partner with each other. That meant the dollar amount requested might be doubled, tripled, or more.

Then again, in a worst-case scenario, the Sharks just wouldn't get the business at all and the contestant could be humiliated in front of as many as 10 million viewers.

Running through my brain were the same head-trips you get before a big final exam. "Nerve-wracking" would be an understatement to describe all the what-ifs: *What if I freeze up and my mind goes blank? What if I forget my major selling points? What if my youth and inexperience turn them off?* Then there was the calming and empowering voice reminding me—*If I do well, it could make a dramatic difference for my start-up and for countless numbers of people who could be helped by what we do.*

Finally, Michael and Allen came running up to tell me they were ready. The doors in front of me slid open.

Deep breath. I walked into the Colosseum, aka the Shark Tank.

Under the bright lights, I did a fast scan of the panel to see which five Sharks were in the house. Glancing from right to left, I identified Robert Herjavec first, then Lori Greiner, with Kevin O'Leary (aka Mr. Wonderful) in the middle, Daymond John next in line, and finally Mark Cuban.

"Hi, Sharks," I began and introduced myself and Scholly, letting them know right off the bat, "I'm seeking $40,000 for 15 percent of my company."

No reaction. So I forged ahead: "College is expensive. I know, I'm a student. The cost of college rises every year. And students and parents are forced to take out student loans to pay the bills. This puts many students in insurmountable debt. But there is an alternative." Dramatic pause.

Still, they gave me nothing.

Not a problem. I had to bait the hook before reeling anyone in. The answer is simple, I said: "Scholarships. The problem is that these scholarships are extremely hard to find. This causes millions of dollars in free money to go to waste, as many students don't know this money exists."

Free money going to waste? The bait dangled.

At last, I detected a hint of curiosity. Lori Greiner, known as the Queen of QVC in tribute to the countless retail products she had launched into the stratosphere through creative marketing strategies, leaned forward. So did Robert Herjavec, who had made his fortune from broad-based investments. Mark Cuban, the only billionaire Shark, owner of the Dallas Mavericks, and an early investor in technology, even gave me a brief smile. Daymond John, the African-American fashion mogul and branding expert who created the global brand FUBU (For Us By Us) by selling T-shirts out of the back of his car at rap concerts, also nodded with slight interest. The one Shark who remained impassive was Kevin O'Leary, sarcastically dubbed Mr. Wonderful for his occasional soft spot for a good pitch despite how easily he could shred a faulty business model or flat out tell an entrepreneur, "You're dead to me," if he was out of the running. An entrepreneur who had brought a Midas touch to everything from software to investment funds, Mr. Wonderful was also notoriously tight with the purse strings—yet brilliant in his intricate deal-making.

The real test came next as I turned to a nearby screen to demonstrate how Scholly worked to match students with hundreds of potential scholarships. "You input information about yourself, touch the state you live in, your GPA, and press 'match' . . . a list of scholarships you qualify for, literally in minutes."

On the screen was a list of fictional scholarships I created to inject some humor and a little sarcasm into the mix. I put up a generous scholarship amount for Lori's "Zero to Hero Scholarship," a very low amount for "Mr. Wonderful's Stingy Scholarship," and so on.

Somebody commented on how bold I was, daring to make jokes at the Sharks' expense.

Almost everyone laughed. Lori Greiner, smiling big, said, "We love you already."

Scowling, Kevin O'Leary disagreed. "Well, you're really sucking up to me," he complained.

Shrugging, I pointed out, "Well, you're stingy, man . . . what can I say?"

Shark-taming lesson #2: *Don't let "them" set the terms of the negotiation just because they're writing the check; be clear on the whole value of what you have to offer.*

That's the clarity I brought to my next point, as I underscored, "Scholly isn't just a business, it's my passion. I want to help students like myself find money to go to the college of their dreams. Investing in Scholly means that you too can help some dreams come true. So let's do this."

Kevin agreed that college was expensive and that it was a real jungle for people trying to find the scholarships. But then, wanting to find a weakness in my model, he asked, "Is that the actual app?"

"Yes," I answered, and he followed up, "How are you curating all the scholarships?"

Besides the archiving that I'd begun in my initial search back in high school and had never stopped, I explained, I was able to aggregate the list from a multitude of websites, and now we no longer had to manage the process manually.

It was Lori who asked about that process and about my cofounders who were the tech-savvy part of our operation. Then Robert Herjavec jumped in, asking how I came up with the idea.

With that, I launched into my own story, mentioning how I'd been wanting to help other students when I got to Drexel and was able to draw from my own struggle and success in winning $1.3 million in scholarships.

Jaws dropped. Robert just said, "What?!" Lori blurted out, "How did you achieve that?" Before I could answer, Mark Cuban commented, "That's like a lottery win."

Even though Daymond and Kevin said less, they both leaned forward when Robert asked where I got the drive to navigate the process. In brief, I admitted how difficult my family situation was and how important it was for me to go away to college. Overcoming the roadblocks was mostly about hard work. "I had a great GPA—I had good test scores. I actually could not apply to some of the schools I wanted to go to because of the application fees."

Robert was quick to say, "I think we can all relate to that story. I'm the first person in my family ever to go to college. I get the value."

Right there, Daymond gave me credit for my Shark-taming skills. "What you just did was amazing. Do you think you could get me $1.3 million for educating these bobos up here for the last five years?"

Now, in pitch mode, refusing to get caught up in Shark drama, I pressed on, "Actually, with Scholly . . . every student that uses the app is matched between 120 and 220 scholarships totaling over $4 million."

Mr. Wonderful clarified that the scholarships found by Scholly were institution-neutral. Right on the money, I confirmed.

Daymond, about to ask a question, was interrupted by Kevin, who asked, "Hey, Christopher, how do I make money with this?"

Ready for that one, I noted how our effective PR strategy (not mentioning that it had been done without capital) had already garnered us 92,000 app downloads, without much cost. When reporters heard about my success as the Million Dollar Scholar, they had a story to write, and it was gaining momentum every day.

In that instant, as Robert declared, "It's brilliant!" I thought: *All right, I've got five Sharks on the line.*

Suddenly, a light turned on in Lori's eyes. Everyone got quiet as she jumped in, saying to me, "Do you know something, Christopher? I'm going to do something that I've never done before. I haven't heard a whole lot, but I'm going to make you an offer right now."

"Awesome."

Mark Cuban, who was just warming up, turned to Lori and said, "Let me just ask some questions, okay?"

Lori ignored that request and focused instead on my reaction as she announced she was prepared to make me an offer right in that moment. Again, Mark tried to get a word in edgewise. "Real questions," he began, but before he could complete his thought, Lori topped him with her offer of exactly what I'd asked for: "The 40k for 15 percent."

The other Sharks shifted in their chairs. This was not Lori's usual style, to be so aggressive early in a pitch. She was now selling herself to me. "I believe in you, I believe what you're doing is good. I think that we will make it to-gether, so I hope that you just say yes."

This was one scenario I hadn't expected. As happy as I was that Lori had championed me and given me exactly what I asked for, I hesitated, making it clear that "I would love to hear other offers, and Lori, I really appreciate that . . . that really means a lot to me. Scholly is very im-portant to me."

Lori nodded. She got it. In fact, she added, "I'm not even going to ask you, 'How do we monetize this?' But I want you to say yes."

Daymond saw me about to answer and then threw his hat in the ring. "I want to be part of this. It's really a personal matter. I started working at ten years old, and I was raised by a single mother. When I got to about seventeen, I wanted to go to college, but I had to go to work, because I saw her working three jobs, and there was no food on the table. I resonate with this. So I'll offer you the same thing. The forty thousand for 15 percent."

Lori intensified her appeal. "Christopher, look at me," she repeated. "I believe in what you are doing, I don't care about how we're going to monetize it. . . . I just want you to take my hand. And say 'deal.' And we will make it work. But I would like you to do it right now."

Kevin O'Leary: "Wow, that's pretty aggressive . . ."

Daymond John: "It's in your best interest to listen to everybody." After a beat, he added, "I just want to be a part of this."

Knowing that Daymond was right about hearing from the whole panel, I insisted, "I just want to hear what everyone has to say," though I reassured Lori, "I love your offer, I love the money."

A rapid-fire series of questions followed. Robert homed in on my ability to update the scholarships and asked if there was a back-end engine for doing that. Mark cut to the chase before I could answer, asking, "How many different scholarships do you have in your database?"

"Between ten and twenty thousand," I answered and started to mention that one of my cofounders had built an algorithm.

Mark Cuban: "Now that's what we're trying to get to. You have two cofounders, they're developers, I want to know what their skillset is."

Robert Herjavec: "Me too, that's what I want to know, how you're going to grow. . . . This could be a very large business."

Lori Greiner (not waiting for me to answer them): "You walked in here with a thought, and Daymond and I both are not even asking you . . ."

Robert: "Let him answer, I want to know what he says."

Lori (not letting Robert get in her way): "You know what? Hang on, hang on."

At this point, a minor Shark spat erupted, as Robert accused Lori: "You're minimizing him, let him answer."

Lori: "I'm not minimizing him!"

Kevin: "Do you want a charity donation, or do you want to build a business?"

Lori: "That's ridiculous!"

Before the spat turned into a real fight, I gave them my bottom line, saying, "I want someone who really believes in what we're doing."

Lori and Daymond chimed in almost in unison that they

each believed in me, while Robert kind of insulted both of them by asking, "How could you believe if you haven't even asked about the entire business?"

Daymond answered that they'd figure it out as they moved on, and if they had issues they'd call Robert with questions.

Finally, Lori took a different tack, offering to partner with Daymond. The two conferred and agreed to go in fifty-fifty. Daymond repeated the offer to me that he and Lori would give $20,000 each and split 15 percent of my company.

Lori came in for the close. "You have to make a decision now."

I looked at the two of them, thrilled to have gotten their combined expertise and the money that I asked for. One of the reasons my ask had been modest was that I didn't want to give up more of a percentage than 15 percent. If the money had gone higher, I might have been tempted to give up more equity.

Shark-taming lesson #3: *Be careful what you ask for because you might just get it.* In this case, I was going to get the combined help of not one but two Sharks. There was no downside.

After a beat I announced, "I'm going to take your deal."

With that, we had a group hug, and I exited the tank ready to bounce off the walls, telling the producers on camera, "I am feeling really great . . . to find two Sharks that think more about what Scholly is going to do for the public than the bottom line. I'm super excited."

Meanwhile, unbeknownst to me, back on the set the Sharks were still circling. When I threw a viewing party in Philly the following February, in 2015, for about two hundred of my closest friends, it was shocking to watch. Previews had billed the segment as promising to include the biggest fight in *Shark Tank* history. That was strange to me because I didn't remember the squabbling getting that bad. But there, on the big screen TV, I watched Robert Herjavec fume as he told Lori and Daymond, "When I had nothing and I couldn't rub two pennies together, you know what I really hated? I hated when people wanted to give me a break . . . because they felt bad for me."

Visibly offended, Lori corrected Robert. "We're not doing it because we feel bad for him."

Daymond echoed her sentiment. "I don't feel bad for him . . . at all."

Robert said he wasn't undermining what they did, but he accused them of not understanding how the back-end engine worked. Daymond shot that down, pointing out that it was clear how much money we made every time the app was downloaded.

Kevin interrupted Daymond. "Is it a charity or is it a business?"

"It's an app that's been downloaded 92,000 times," Daymond repeated from earlier. He emphasized that, with little overhead, we were already a profitable start-up—with millions more to be made.

Robert couldn't get off his argument and directed his words at Lori, complaining, "I'm a very charitable guy too."

"Sometimes," Lori schooled Robert, "it's about helping America and making the world a better place."

Robert actually said, "Lori, that is such crap."

Lori, up in arms, shot back, "No, it is not crap."

Robert was adamant. "We are not the charity tank."

The disgruntled Sharks kept complaining that Lori and Daymond must have been doing a charity deal because they didn't know the ins and outs of Scholly yet. They were barking questions like "How does it work?" and "How are you going to grow that business?" and "What's the execution plan?"

As I watched all of this unfold at the viewing party those many months later, I had to laugh. On the one hand, Scholly was booming, and after this broadcast our subscriber base would shoot up from the hundred thousands to the millions—at the same time that our services increased and we moved to a monthly subscription fee of $2.99. And the fight itself was only lifting our profile. Absolutely, the Legend of the Big Break had come true *and* all those smaller earlier breaks had made it possible.

But something troubled me about the fight playing out on-screen.

Toward the end, Robert assured Lori, "I'm not trying to give you a hard time."

Lori scoffed at that. "You guys just don't like it when you get scooped."

Mark Cuban took offense, and the other two tried to interrupt her again as she said, "Wait, wait, excuse me, I'm talking. . . . The bottom line is, you guys, I actually believe that Daymond and I, no matter what it is that this guy needs, we'll be there to back him up. It's not the charity tank."

At last, Robert lost it and said to Lori, "You know what, you are really pissing me off right now. I'm going to say something rude to you. . . . I don't want to say something rude to you."

"No," she stopped him, "you're not, because you are not a rude guy."

Instead of saying anything rude, Robert got up from his seat and started to walk off, leaving Lori flabbergasted. She told him, "You're not the guy to walk away and walk off." She added, "Yes, we're the Shark Tank and we're not the charity tank. But sometimes there is a point to being compassionate and caring."

Kevin went for one last gnashing of his teeth and said they had killed me by choking me on the $40,000. He then walked off.

Mark Cuban was still arguing that they could have

given me $100,000 if "you want to help him and all these kids and send a message . . ."

Lori stopped him. "I feel great about what I did."

Daymond echoed her: "I feel great."

With nothing else to say, Mark followed the other two off the set. The three white men had now walked off the set, leaving two Sharks who happened to be (1) a person of color and (2) a woman.

Later, Kevin O'Leary told CNBC that my pitch had been the most masterful he had ever seen, and that everyone who was ever going to go on *Shark Tank* should study everything I did because I had them all hooked from the start.

Wow. And yet the optics weren't great. Three white men walking away because they couldn't control the narrative—because, as Lori pointed out, they'd somehow had their power taken away, while the one woman and the one African-American on the panel were the ones eager to embrace a business that was larger in scope than its bottom line.

Yet this was my proof of concept for my life—that going where there was no path had been the right thing to do all along. This was leveling up in a quantum way.

The reality for me and for Scholly is that *Shark Tank* exposed us to millions of potential users. Almost overnight, we became the number-one overall app in both the iOS App Store and the Google Play Store for over three weeks.

Some start-ups never achieve that stature, yet for us it was only the beginning. Something had happened that was as important as our sales. For me, it was a rite of passage. Instead of being chewed up and spat out by the Sharks, I tamed them and got at least two of them to agree that the new paradigm of social entrepreneurship could be viable and profitable.

The experience helped me realize that, in one form or another, I'd been trying to tame potential foes and turn them into allies for most of my life. Shark-taming is what we all have to do whenever we go up against preconceived ideas about who we are and what we are capable of achieving.

There's a question that is often asked in marketing, PR, and promotional circles: *Would you prefer to have a campaign that's a microwave or a crockpot?* If your campaign is a microwave, you blow up right away and get a lot of attention, which puts you on the map at a level that your competition can't attain. The challenge with the microwave campaign is the reality that your success may be unsustainable if more success doesn't follow. A crockpot campaign, on the other hand, is a slow cook that kind of bubbles up and gets nice and warm over a long period of time.

My feeling is that it's good for a campaign to be a little of both. A crockpot approach lets you build and grow at a steady pace, enabling those inflection points to happen when you level up. And a microwave approach can bring on a well-timed massive disruption that provides exposure and connection like nothing else. To run both a crockpot and a microwave campaign, look to your brand—and its durability, its versatility, and the community that makes it matter.

If becoming a brand, founding a start-up, or sparking a movement isn't something you've thought possible or within the realm of attainable for you, my next chapter may change your mind.

Chapter 8

The New Networking Paradigm

IT TAKES A VILLAGE TO BUILD A LASTING BRAND

The currency of real networking is not greed but generosity.

—Keith Ferrazzi, entrepreneur and author

Earlier, you may recall, I talked about the question of HOW I overcame growing up in an environment that didn't give me access to opportunity, and the power of questions that begin with HOW. The thinking behind that word requires us to engage our problem-solving skills—even for big issues that lead to solutions impacting not just ourselves but others. Clearly, the question "How am I going to pay for college?" was about as powerful as any question I could have ever asked.

The beauty of questions that begin with HOW is that

they get your brain going in a positive, practical, answer-driven mode. Of course, posing a question that begins with a HOW doesn't mean other questions of WHO, WHAT, WHERE, WHEN, WHY, and HOW MUCH are somehow insignificant.

On the contrary.

Say, for example, you are gathering data about WHERE to go to college. Or you are making the leap after graduation into the working world and are unsure about WHEN the best time might be to go apply for a job or HOW MUCH you can expect to be paid, or WHAT you need to do to connect to investment opportunities or potential partners in a business you'd like to launch.

When you are moving into any daunting next field of unknowns, choices, options, and uncertainties that require you to answer all these different questions, the one that is often most overlooked is WHO. I'm not sure why that is, because in almost every success story told by the most influential entrepreneurs and thought leaders there is always a recognition of certain people who played a meaningful role in their journey.

Sometimes in our desire for independence or to avoid following the conventional route, we may resist allowing anyone else to give us too much input or to influence our choices too much. Sometimes we rely too much on the advice and opinions of the friends, parents, mentors, and other people we know or happen to meet.

Either way, I would still argue that when it comes to moving forward with dreams and goals, the old saying holds true: "It's not *what* you know but *who* you know that matters." You could also say that as you set your sights on getting a foothold in certain arenas, it's not *what* you'd like to know but *who* you'd like to know.

Let's say you're applying to colleges and you want to be a theater major. You'd like to have a conservatory training experience but also be able to get a well-rounded liberal arts education. You've auditioned and applied and been accepted to three of your choices—Carnegie Mellon in Pittsburgh, New York University's Tisch School in New York City, and Bennington College in Vermont. Congratulations are first in order. Clearly, you're talented, and each of these schools has a terrific theater program! Ideally, you'll be able to go visit each of the three campuses and have a chance to meet with some of the professors. You can also read their bios and look at the course schedules to see what they teach. Perhaps even more helpful, a campus visit will give you the opportunity to meet current students and get a vibe that may answer the question: *Do these folks feel like "my people"? Can I see myself hanging out with fellow students here and being a part of this community?*

If you can't physically visit a campus, there are usually alumni who would be happy to tell you about what their experiences were, what the social life was like, and how easy or hard it was to balance fun, learning, extracurricular activities, and, if relevant, on-campus employment. The more people you can interview, the better sense you'll get of the *culture* and *character* of that institution.

Some people go so far as to say that the peers you meet and befriend in college are the most likely to become your extended family in years to come, even for the rest of your life. For that reason, feeling that you align with the culture and character of the place where you intend to spend four years or more is a must. There are other considerations. It's always important to like the geographic location of where you decide to enroll. You know yourself. Do you want change or familiarity? Do you like to be in the middle of a big city or out in a natural setting? Do you want a self-contained campus that you don't leave very often, or do you want proximity to other campuses and to cultural and recreational outlets? Do you want to live in a dorm throughout your college tenure, or would you be happy living in off-campus housing? The answers to questions like these should help determine your pick. More important, though, are the questions about the people who will be studying there with you, along with the teaching and administrative staff.

For anyone who is on the all-important job hunt—whether you've just graduated or you've been out of college for a while or you're changing lanes down the road—your WHO is going to matter more than ever. The statistics I've seen most recently say that between 60 and 80 percent of job hires are the result of networking. Plus, as many as 70 percent of all currently employed people would like to have another job.

If you boil that down, it tells you that (a) applying for jobs only via online submissions puts you at a disadvantage, and (b) if you are entering the working world for the first time, you may be at an even greater disadvantage with so many already employed individuals (with work experience) competing for the same jobs as you.

Clearly, with the competition as tough as it is, just throwing your résumé into the mix could be considered a proverbial crapshoot. Knowing someone who can help open a door or knowing someone who knows someone with an inside track can make all the difference in the world.

Assuming that you are a fairly social person, one of your first moves might be to connect to friends and fellow grads from your alma mater. Most private and many public universities offer you access to alumni lists, complete with contact information for networking. Don't hesitate to reach out. You may think that you're bothering a stranger to ask for a favor but that's only partly true. For one thing, you have a common connection already, so you can't be total strangers. For another, if you give someone an opportunity to open a door for you, either in this one instance or with some ongoing advice and mentoring, their help and your success will reflect on both of you and on the institution you both attended.

If you attended a large university and it still feels awkward making a random call or sending an email to someone just because they went to the same institution, look for smaller networks among the alumni lists. For example, many of the associations, social clubs, fraternities/sororities, and service organizations you join while in college have active networks you can tap and that can even connect you nationally to affiliated networks.

While this may seem like an obvious approach, it's one that's often overlooked. In billionaire investor Ray Dalio's praiseworthy book *Principles*, he actually makes a point of writing, "There are so many new Harvard graduates that underuse or totally ignore the Harvard alumni network." He's not just talking to new grads or Harvard alums. The takeaway for me is a reminder that we forget to harness and cultivate the energy of existing networks and communities.

The art of networking—which starts with identifying the main WHO's WHO in your life and work—has been something of a mystery to a lot of people I meet. Maybe it's being from the South, or the fact that I am pretty outgoing, but to me the best efforts come from totally being your authentic self and having no problem going up to strangers and asking, "Where are *y'all* from?" Or your version of that.

The most artful networking is not to be artful at all—just to be yourself as you engage with another human being and lose the idea that you have to have an agenda.

Then again, there's nothing wrong with having an

agenda as long as you are authentic, direct, and purposeful in your approach. Better yet is when you meet someone and maybe get excited about what you can do to help them, instead of being a climber who looks to meet people based on their ability to help you get somewhere you can't on your own. When you get to know someone else's value as a cool human being, you've made an honest connection and probably found an alignment of your values and interests.

Best of all is when you network with others with the goal of becoming a connector. That is powerful. That's how you build a better network.

Becoming a connector falls under the heading for me of becoming the change you'd like to see. Instead of focusing on what others can do for you—on what you hope to get from them—put your focus on what you can do for them or what you can offer them. Whether or not you get what you want from others becomes moot because you will have found your strength. If you want mentorship, become a mentor. If you want increased opportunity and prosperity, increase someone else's opportunity and prosperity. If you want to belong to a network that lifts you up, bring someone else into your circle and lift them up.

If you want to have certain kinds of people in your personal and work lives, there's nothing wrong with having a conscious awareness of WHO they might be. This isn't about being exclusionary, limited, or judgmental; it's more about getting in touch with your own values. For example,

I love knowing individuals from all walks of life who are energized, motivated, and interested in lots of things—the more diverse from one another and from me, the better.

When you do have a feel for the WHO you'd like to know, you tend to find them. Or they find you. In my experience, the connection is instantaneous, and most are like-minded people who give you a sense of belonging and of being at home right away.

When I was growing up and feeling like an overly bookish nerd, I found my WHOs on the pages of comic books—other nerds who doubled as superheroes. When I started reading the stories of the original founders of Silicon Valley and the tech industry, I felt a sense of kinship right off. Entrepreneurial success on a massive level helped to rebrand anyone who had ever been labeled a geek or a nerd.

Bill Gates had long been my hero, even before I won the Millennium Scholarship award. One of the most validating, motivational statements he ever made was when he famously said, "Be nice to nerds. Chances are you'll end up working for one."

Not all my important relationships are with people who were former or are current nerds. Rather, I think of our commonality as about being self-possessed, confident in who we are, and in one way or another carving out our own paths. We may come from totally different backgrounds and have different personality types. At the same time, despite differences, there are moments when you're networking and you click with someone immediately—so much so you feel like you don't have to tell your story. They get you right away. You're sympatico. You tend to laugh at the same jokes and are concerned about similar issues.

Granted, not everybody is a social animal. You may not feel comfortable introducing yourself to folks you don't know at all. The reality is that in this time more and more of us work remotely and have fewer opportunities to meet people organically in social settings. So we all have to switch up how we connect and expand our networks.

Not long ago I read a top business blog's list of do's and don'ts for networking and was shocked to see how outdated they seemed. In their pre-pandemic thinking, the authors still felt they had to emphasize the importance of looking into someone's eyes and giving them a firm handshake. Obviously, though, when you connect with someone you don't know well, it's important to try to get a sense of WHO that person is.

Again, sizing them up should not be for the self-serving reason of figuring out whether they can help *you* in some way, but whether you can help *them*. Connecting to a new friend should be more organic. Maybe this is someone who likes the same music you do, or who wants to invite you to meet his or her friends, or who shares an interest in supporting a charitable cause that you support. Maybe you have a project or service that aligns with something someone else he or she knows is working on. Or vice versa.

This new paradigm of networking is a departure from our old practices based on establishing a market commodity exchange—you do this for me, and I'll do this for you, in what we think of as *transactional* relationships. The new paradigm is what thought leaders like Keith Ferrazzi call relationships aimed at *mutual elevation.*

When you begin to think in terms of WHO would elevate you and WHO you could elevate, you're creating more than a network—you're creating a community. And rather than *transactional*, the networking watchwords are *mutually supportive, complementary*, and *collaborative.*

The new paradigm, in my view, creates a community that is interactive and enriches and empowers its members, who, for the most part, share similar values. In my network, for instance, one common bond is the value we put on education and its connection to access and elevation professionally.

As I've gotten older, I have to say, my sense of this new paradigm of networking is as simple as wanting to be surrounded by good people. By that I mean people who are good to you, and good for your soul.

From the time I formed a company while still at Drexel and had to grow it quickly, with good people I could help and good people helping me, that understanding has served me well.

Creating community is rewarding personally, and it's also just smart business. For me, becoming a connector led to connections that have helped me bring a sense of family to my work and find a secure position in the world outside of college—which can be a very scary place for those of us leaving the nest of a second home away from home that college represents.

When you go off on the pathless route, no matter how much of a maverick or rugged individualist you are, your network can be your X factor that determines your success or lack thereof.

When others are invested in your success and you in theirs, magic happens.

Without question, the introduction of Scholly to the world on a mass media scale changed the app's trajectory—and mine. The whirlwind it created was so swift and sudden that I had to scramble to graduate in time.

During the airing of my episode on *Shark Tank* in February 2015, I looked around at the couple hundred friends from Philly watching with me and remembered the kid from Birmingham who had arrived here four and a half years earlier, knowing no one. The contrast was a validation of how fortunate I was to have landed at Drexel. Between the communications and business schools, as well as my friends and mentors from the University of Pennsylvania and the Dorm Room Fund communities, I'd formed lasting relationships on various fronts. Many of my first hires for Scholly had come from this network, and most of them are still with the company today.

Before graduation, Scholly had opened an office in downtown Philadelphia, and we had hired a chief operating officer and a chief marketing officer—both very experienced and older than me. My mentors had encouraged me to hire people who were smarter than me and had expertise to offer in the running of a company.

You might think that's what any young founder/CEO would do. If you're twenty-three years old, it's essential to know what you don't know. Still, it's not always easy for younger founders to listen and defer to the wisdom of others who they might think don't have their finger on the same pulse of the business. This issue was addressed in a 2008 *Harvard Business Review* article by Noam Wasserman, author of *The Founder's Dilemmas: Anticipating and Avoiding the Pitfalls That Can Sink a Startup*. Wasserman observes:

> Many entrepreneurs are overconfident about their prospects and naive about the problems they will face. . . . Founders' attachment, overconfidence, and naïveté may be necessary to get new ventures up and running, but these emotions later create problems.

Not much has changed in the years since Wasserman made these points. The most recent analysis I've seen (www.failory.com) as to why 90 percent of start-ups fail cites such common causes as a lack of product or market fit (34 percent; companies with this issue didn't learn the important lesson that product is king), marketing failures (22 percent), human resource/team problems (18 percent), and financial problems (16 percent). Other, less common causes of failure include legal, operational, or tech problems.

When I sat down with our CMO and COO, I looked for their guidance as far as how to avoid the usual pitfalls and other areas of weakness. They came back with great advice. In essence they recommended that before we addressed our potential weaknesses, it was a good idea to identify and build on the strengths that had brought us so far so quickly.

This is a step that's often overlooked, both in business and in our personal lives. While we're busy fixing, improving, troubleshooting, innovating, and disrupting, we forget to look at where we are and pay attention to the strengths that have helped us achieve milestones. Improvement and adopting strategies to avoid pitfalls still matter. First, though, do your strength assessment so you don't throw the baby out with the bathwater.

The four things that helped us build the brand early on included:

1. *My personal scholarship search story.* My story of looking for money to pay for college and discovering money that was looking for students was a classic proof of concept, and it anchored the brand from then on.
2. *Speed.* The fact that I move fast normally and then was early to market with a great idea underscored the urgency of the solution that Scholly presented.
3. *Repeat exposure.* Learning the basics of PR and crafting a finely tuned elevator pitch led to exposure that built from local to regional to national. Meticulous preparation for media appearances was key, especially on *Shark Tank*. Nothing was left to chance.
4. *Untraditional networking.* This was more true to my style versus any well-designed plan. Yet taking an unconventional approach to networking, seeking connections to communities, paid off from the start.

Knowing your strengths can make it easier to address shortcomings and consciously work to avoid the usual pitfalls that can trip up any founder/CEO or spearheader of a project. More than anything, know ahead of time that if you seek to rise to a position of power and influence, the force that will carry you there is respect. And you can underline the following: <u>Respect can't be expected or demanded. Respect has to be earned.</u>

Many founders who become CEOs have trouble giving

up control of the company they created and unrealistically expect employees or equity holders to defer to them. You can't expect members of your team to respect you because of the title you gave to yourself as the entrepreneur. You may well be the face of the brand, but once you build a team and open your doors for commerce, everyone is a stakeholder. Your greatest assets, I have learned, are the people who share your passion, hard work, hustle, grit, scholarship, and faith and who all recognize the need to partner in working toward a common goal.

My team reflects a departure from the hiring practices of most tech companies. Close to 99 percent of Scholly employees are people of color with women outnumbering men. Throughout my life, my most influential mentors have been women, so I have made it a priority to hire and promote strong female executives. We incentivize success through collaboration and reward excellence, initiative, and great results.

After my co-op experience at Fannie Mae with a boss who disregarded the opinions of a lowly intern like me, I had made up my mind to be respectful of all input once I ran my own shop. That became a priority at Scholly—to listen and create dialogue around ways to do the two things that start-ups are supposed to do: (1) grow the business (in revenue and users) and (2) innovate. My priority was to create a safe space for everyone to feel empowered to contribute ideas that might improve our brand, our reach, our efficiency, and our productivity. Ultimately, the decision to act or not to act on those ideas would be up to me.

There is a simple way to earn the respect of others, and that is by respecting and trusting them. That was not hard to do, especially because I knew to surround myself with smart, detail-oriented people. The challenge for me, as it is for many upper-level executives, was learning to delegate and not micromanage. When you're used to grinding and juggling multiple task lists (and not always well), it's hard to let go and accept that you've hired people who can handle some of the load for you.

Once I improved at delegating, I freed myself up to do my work as the public face of Scholly and to grow our brand vision. My cofounders, especially Nick, who served as our chief technical officer, were then able to focus on making sure that our technological infrastructure could support that growth.

And therein lay a challenge. One of the lesser-understood reasons that some technology companies succeed at such a massive scale is that once the tech infrastructure is in place, it's meant to be able to accommodate unlimited numbers of users without costing more and more. If you compare tech to manufacturing, where success requires expansion of factories and retail outlets, the advantage of hitting it big in tech is easy to see. That, however, doesn't tell the whole story. Technology requires maintenance and improvement, and that requires money.

In theory I knew that the more we grew, the more funding we would need to grow staff and refine technology to support and service more users. Not much could have prepared me for that dramatic reality. To say that I was overwhelmed would be an understatement.

Shortly after *Shark Tank*, not only did we strike gold with individual users, but thanks to new relationships and constant networking we hit another marketing bonanza with institutional sales.

When the Drexel University financial aid office decided to purchase a block of downloads for students seeking additional funding, I thought it was a kind of onetime thing, that they were doing it just because they knew me and were happy to support the app. Then I got a call from my longtime mentor, Dr. Karen Starks, about the possibility of giving a block of Scholly downloads to students at South Gwinnett High School in Georgia, where she'd been volunteering.

Touched, I assumed she meant twenty or so downloads, but when I started to put through the order and asked for the exact amount, Dr. Starks answered, "Let's do six hundred."

"Six hundred?" I was thrilled.

She explained that there were six hundred seniors in the high school, and that many of them had never thought about going on to college because of the cost. She couldn't just give that opportunity to some of the students and not to others.

After the purchase went through and she'd had a chance to witness students logging in to the app for the first time, she reported, close to tears, "You should have seen their faces when they started seeing that they qualified for twenty, thirty, forty scholarships—some students got over 150 hits right off!"

Dr. Starks generated more press by telling a reporter, "Scholly is changing what students think that they can achieve. They have proof that says: 'There may be help out there; I can reach that goal.'"

Soon a wave of other teachers and financial aid offices followed suit. Then a math teacher from Memphis, Tennessee—who was also a city councilman—caused an even bigger stir when he decided, "I wanted Memphis to be the first city in the nation to have Scholly for its school system." To pay for it, he spearheaded a fundraising drive, promoting the idea of creating opportunity and access for all Memphis students.

His activism and stance inspired me and made me realize that as much as we founders think we are the ones to define our brands, in truth it takes a village to build a relevant and enduring brand. This was the first time I had heard my vision of creating a product that provided access for all articulated by an adopter of it.

This raises two further points to consider about branding practices. First, your business's WHO, all its stakeholders, contributes to what your brand can be second only to you. My second point for founders, entrepreneurs, and activists is that your personal brand should not overshadow the brand of your company or your cause.

It took me a while to recognize the need for the separation. Sometimes the lines are murky too. For example, in my journey as a spokesperson and media figure, my focus is on being a social entrepreneur—a businessman with a social impact. This applies to Scholly, of course. However, knowing that the day might come when an acquisition offer to buy Scholly might make sense, I wouldn't want to be so inextricably linked to it that no one else could take over. We did, in fact, have some early offers that were tempting—especially when I was feeling overwhelmed by the challenge of learning to run a company while running it. In the end, the timing was never right, and I said no often enough that the industry got the message that I wasn't interested in selling.

The good news was that I was careful to build my own story separate from Scholly's and to seek exposure that was less about me and more about the impact the app was having on users' lives.

On social media and in person, I am known for my directness, even bluntness. I am not afraid to say what I feel, to be honest and unapologetic. When I speak out against poverty, against homophobia and racism, when I go against the popular grain, those are my views. Having a distinct personal brand story is also my way of trying to avoid being turned into a mythical creature when my aspiration is to be someone who has a social impact and to inspire others to know their potential for impact.

Just as you thought about your personal strengths and attributes when applying to college, for scholarships, and for jobs, you can take a similar inventory for your personal brand—for how you present yourself in social media.

One reason I'm purposeful about self-branding is so as not to be pigeonholed or expected to fall in with prevailing views and actions. My brand reflects my southern roots, my (sometimes sarcastic) sense of humor, my authentic Blackness, my cultural pride, and the fact that I'm out as a young Black entrepreneur who is also a nerd. How I express WHO I am is to promote Black excellence, using vernacular if it's honest, but not because that's going to make me cool or hip or more woke. My favorite hashtag is #blackboyjoy.

Having a personal brand usually means that you intend to become or already have become *known for something*. Similarly, your business's brand crystallizes when the company has become *known for something*. That's where exposure can make you or break you.

There is a saying that all press is good press. Not so. Bad press is bad press, and when you are in business, bad press can hurt you, your company brand, and your network. That was something that hit home for me in connection with the deal that we struck with the city of Memphis. How that came about is a story worth telling as a cautionary tale.

A couple of months before my graduation from Drexel, I was unbelievably excited to take part in the kickoff ceremonies, press conference, and celebration of a successful funding campaign for Scholly. As Memphis is not a long drive from Birmingham, I invited my mother up to Memphis to attend the press conference with the mayor, city council members, school board officials, and members of law enforcement.

We had not really had great communication in those years, but I had certainly paid homage to her whenever possible. This seemed like something I could share with her, and I booked a hotel room for her so she could stay the night.

A short while before the press conference was scheduled to start, Momma, married at the time and in her thirties, showed up with another man, who was not someone I felt comfortable including in the ceremonies.

"Oh," she said nonchalantly, pointing to the guy, "you've met before."

I felt that Momma should have known this would irk me, but somehow she seemed not to care. That's when I finally understood that she probably had no frame of reference for the impact of education on me, nor for the magnitude of this event. During the time that I was developing Scholly, she and I had rarely communicated, so it may have been difficult for her to relate to how my experiences had changed me.

For years, on my own and in therapy, I had tried to make sense of loved ones who I felt lacked the critical thinking capacity that comes with education, literacy, and resources for dealing with psychological issues. I knew Momma was childlike, even at thirty-seven, but at that moment in time the last thing I wanted was drama interrupting a ceremony meant to honor me and my team. I was afraid she had no concept of what I'd worked so hard to achieve.

When I asked to speak to her in private, she seemed insulted. "What's your problem?"

We went to the hotel room I'd reserved for her, as I explained that the press might want to interview her and it was inappropriate to have this man with her. Probably I added that I'd looked forward to introducing her to my cofounder and others who were there to cheer me on. Not anymore.

Momma muttered something about me being inappropriate.

What did she mean by that? At that moment I had no clue.

Over the next few weeks, as I thought about it, I figured her comment was a dis about my recently coming out. Rightly or wrongly, I took it as a rejection of me, and it was painful. She was the person who had given me life, after all, and I couldn't process it—other than to think she was unhappy that I had criticized her and was striking back.

That's what I was feeling when I told her, "You need to leave." And she got in her car with the boyfriend, and they drove out of there to go back to Birmingham in time for me to gather my composure and join the press conference.

Everything went really well, although I was heart-broken inside. The coverage was fantastic, fortunately, and before long I found myself traveling more and more to Washington, DC—visiting the White House, testifying in front of Congress on education policy, and expanding the Scholly network exponentially. Soon we were in talks with the state of Montana to arrange for sales of the app to every high school senior in the state. A short while after that, I was invited to join the Obama Foundation's My Brother's Keeper project and was named Ernst and Young's Entrepreneur of the Year for 2015 for Philadelphia.

Those were indeed heady experiences that I tried to take in stride and also to savor.

In the weeks after our encounter in Memphis, Momma did ask about attending my graduation at Drexel. By then, it was too late. Sad as it may sound, she never had a hand in my college education, and it didn't make sense for her to show up for my celebration.

The last time we saw each other was in that hotel room in Memphis in 2015. I had not really understood how far my own path had taken me from where I began. There was no going back. Sometimes you have to cut ties.

Scholly was my family now, and Philadelphia my adopted home. Incredibly, when we officially incorporated in 2015, our rollout read like a fairy tale. The only concern—though it wasn't fatal—was our failure to attract much if any venture capital. Money was tight, despite our growing exposure.

This was a crockpot of a problem, and one I had to try to unplug. The usual way to go was to head to Silicon Valley and score big. Shockingly, I couldn't even get a meeting. The excuses were many, but they all boiled down to lack of access, lack of connection. How bad was it? Let's just say that if you looked at a list of the one hundred top tech founders and entrepreneurs of the last forty years, only two would be women, only two would be Black, and only a handful would be immigrants.

Gaining access to Silicon Valley for Scholly wasn't going to happen. But it turned out that Silicon Valley was going to come to me.

A lot of folks assume that once you get the investment the Sharks come in, take over, and run your business for you.

Happily, that wasn't the case for Scholly. Lori and Daymond were wonderful in terms of lending their expertise, but they were not intrusive. The one issue they really pressed was "You need to change the business model." In other words, we had to raise the price. Bottom line: if we were going to be a for-profit company and make all of us money so we could do more to create more access for more users, we were going to have to raise the price.

This was something that my cofounders and I had known we would need to do at some point, but we had kicked that can down the road. All of our advisers—from our executives to the Sharks to mentors like Josh Kopelman and Chuck Sacco—were in agreement. The problem was that in getting a lot of early exposure for the onetime 99 cent download (including in the *USA Today* feature), the brand had been perceived as heroic and a force for good. So an increase in cost could hurt the brand. In fact, we were criticized a lot when we later changed the business model to a monthly recurring $2.99 subscription, with a subsequent optional annual premium fee. However, thanks to networking and the evolution of the Scholly community, we had grown in other ways—with answers to questions that got us to think about how we would offer added value to our subscribers.

A couple of major lessons were there for the taking. First, this was another reminder that it does take a village to create and sustain the vitality of a brand. Again, I was reminded of the different histories of founders who spent a lot of time building up their personal brand and forgot to shine a light on their family of customers. The most infamous brand story was Pepsi goading Coca-Cola into coming up with "New Coke"—a marketing fiasco done without consulting Coke's devoted consumers. The brand survived as soon as it reverted to "Classic Coke."

As the CEO and face of Scholly, I knew the power of my story to inspire audiences to appreciate the need for the app. But if my team and I couldn't demonstrate how the app was raising hundreds of thousands (to date millions) for our users to make their college dreams come true, the brand couldn't continue its relevance.

The other realization I had was that there was still a lot of confusion about what social entrepreneurship really is. That helped explain the hesitation on the part of venture capitalists.

The lack of diversity among Silicon Valley's main players inspired none other than AOL founder Steve Case to go out and fund small tech hubs in cities outside of the major ones already established. In an act of social entrepreneurship, not straight-out philanthropy, he had created Rise of the Rest, a tech contest with huge rewards, to promote opportunity for diverse founders and to invest in underdeveloped and opportunity-rich terrains.

Steve Case, an iconic founder for sure, explained that he believed in the profitability and importance of diversity because investing in "diverse entrepreneurs means solving more diverse problems." The contest in Philly was an all-day pitch competition.

The prize? $100,000.

When the competitors saw me and my partners walking in, I admit, they looked panic-stricken. My main worry was that we would be too polished, too confident, and seemingly too far along to need the prize money. I could have tamped down my confidence or tried to act greener. But it would have been inauthentic. Instead, I just talked about how grateful I was that we had come as far as we had without venture capital and described how much further we could go if we had the means to grow our team and offer more services.

At the end of the pitch day, after some tense minutes of waiting, we learned that Scholly had won and that we had the blessing of Steve Case. We now were in an even more illustrious network that you might call "Silicon Valley–adjacent." A second $100,000 loan/investment followed, this one from Josh Kopelman.

If my story tells you anything, it hopefully is an echo of where we began—lead with the good and the money will follow. Sometimes it doesn't come the way you are told that it should. To this day, we have not made more than $400,000 from venture capital. My colleagues, many of whom never gained enough traction for their start-ups to become profitable, have still managed to raise millions in venture capital. At one point I would have been envious. In time I came to the conclusion that those millions do the same thing that PR and exposure do—except that you may ultimately give up equity, control, and eventual profits by being beholden to the VCs.

Looking back, I'm grateful for everything that happened and for how it happened, even when obstacles were thrown up that forced us to innovate in order to overcome them. More than anything, I'm grateful to everyone who was the WHO's WHO at different stages of my life.

My challenge to you is to think about the handful of people who have been pivotal in your journey to date and show them some love. If you don't have that handful yet, challenge yourself to go out and make some new connections.

When feeling shy, you can always borrow the words of my Big Ma—"When you can't find the way, make the way."

Chapter 9

Changing the Game

WHY BLACK-OWNED BUSINESSES AND
THE EMPOWERING OF ENTREPRENEURS OF COLOR
(AND WOMEN) SHOULD MATTER TO EVERYONE

Aspiring entrepreneurs have to actually do something that they feel strongly passionate about, and in most cases they should seek inspiration from their own experience. . . . If you had a terrible experience, you should despise the experience to the extent that you are continuously seeking a solution for it.

—Best Ayiorwoth, social entrepreneur
and founder of Girls Power Micro-Lending Organisation
(GIPOMO), supporting loans to woman entrepreneurs
so their daughters can remain in school

From the moment I first conceived of writing a book about forging your own path and leaving a trail for others—an idea that struck in the middle of the Chicago Scholly Summit held during the Snowpocalypse of 2018—I assumed like most of us that the quote on which this book is based had come from Ralph Waldo Emerson. When I went to do some research, though, I quickly learned that he might not have been the originator of that line. To the best of my knowledge, references to going where there is no path are nowhere to be found in any of Emerson's writings. The website Quote Investigator cites one version of the line in a poem from 1903 by Muriel Strode: "I will not follow where the path may lead, but I will go where there is no path, and I will leave a trail."

That same year the line, slightly tweaked, was used in a song by a minister during his sermon at a Unitarian church service. In a 1914 speech, inventor Alexander Graham Bell gave his interpretation of going where there is no path:

> Don't keep forever on the public road, going only where others have *gone* and following one after the other like a flock of sheep. Leave the beaten track occasionally and dive into the woods. Every time you do so you will be certain to find something that you have never seen before.

Apparently, it was in the 1980s that Ralph Waldo Emerson began to be cited as the originator of the line. Maybe he said it in a lecture he gave and the documentation has been lost. For that reason, Muriel Strode has provisionally been credited as the originator of the line.

Alexander Graham Bell's concept of getting off the main

road and diving into the woods from time to time is appealing. So is the hope that our strides can be seen as helping others—when we "leave a trail behind."

HOW we can best choose to do that and the WHYs that each of us need to find to do so—individually and collectively—are the main subjects for this last chapter. The challenges facing all of us right now are unprecedented and apocryphal—which means, we all have to mutually elevate one another by raising our game and changing it.

Many of these challenges have been simmering for years, if not centuries. If ever there was a time for social entrepreneurship, it would be now. If ever there was a generation ready to get off the main road and forge a new way, I believe Millennials and soon members of the Gen Z age group are ready to step up.

Before I talk about what makes me think so, let me catch you up on the coming-of-age of Scholly.

Growing up poor allowed me, in the words of African social entrepreneur Best Ayiorwoth, to "despise the experience to the extent that you are continuously seeking a solution for it."

As a young person, I didn't just check out books on financial literacy; I set up shop by giving my mom and other family members tips on how to be financially literate. It was pretty hilarious when you think about it—a kid explaining to adults how they could improve their credit scores. My first rule of thumb was "Invest first, spend later."

Most of the grown people around me would laugh, saying, "Invest what?"

Then I'd suggest, "You want to put your money to work for you to have what's called passive income." We'd go over options that included high-yield savings accounts that offered 2 percent returns on savings deposits and even higher rates for money market accounts. My second suggested rule was to get three secure credit cards. In other words, when you have some cash, you deposit that amount in a savings account and set up a credit card with the same bank. The thing is, big businesses exploit your lack of education about how banking works and get rich on your debt. Instead, you can game the credit systems by getting those secure cards. They don't care how much or how little you pay. My third rule is to make a plan so that your kids have some assets. Even if you don't have kids yet, it's never too early to start to plan for how you're going to have money to leave to them. My fourth rule—a recommendation really—is to read more for recreation. You don't have to be a consummate reader, but I'm a firm believer that when you read, you change your own life and the lives of others.

One memorable instance was when I was in the seventh grade and my mother had just received her income tax return. Most people would rush to the store to buy something they didn't truly need and blow it all. Right before that happened, I suggested to my mom, "Momma, instead of spending the check on a bunch of stuff we don't need right away, why don't you use your income tax check to go pay your rent ahead of time?"

She laughed like I was crazy.

"But you'll never be behind on your bills."

Then my mother relented, went to pay the rent ahead of time, and for the next year we were never behind, not for one month. For one year we didn't have to worry about finances.

When Scholly was cash-strapped, I budgeted with similarly simple but effective rules to tide us over until money was coming in. Once it did, with an influx of millions, I was equipped to work with our COO to make sure our investments went the furthest. So instead of worrying about Silicon Valley, my solution was to put my energy into other outlets—like developing strategic partnerships and alliances with more cities, states, lawmakers, corporations, and nonprofits in order to widen access to Scholly at the citywide and even statewide level.

In 2016, once we did change the business model to a monthly subscription fee of $2.99, new wheels of innovation began to turn that added value to those subscriptions. One of the concerns for all of us was that once our subscribers applied for scholarships for their first year, we'd see a batch of subscriptions being shut down. The problem I was obsessed with solving was coming up with a way to keep our users for life. The only business model I could find that made sense for Scholly to borrow from was Netflix. It's a classic example of a brand that stayed competitive by going where the path didn't lead—not only leaving Blockbuster back in the dustbin of VHS and DVD rentals but departing from brick-and-mortar stores and switching to direct mail of rentals.

Before anybody had thought about streaming content to their television sets, Netflix had leaned over and looked ahead down the road and developed original content. Subscribers who come on board for a particular series are caught when they get curious about watching another original series or checking out the made-for-Netflix documentaries and reality shows. Netflix has made some stumbles, including the decision to over-index in paying for book rights not yet developed. Nonetheless, I saw its brand identity as being a welcoming place for the entire spectrum of age groups and envisioned the ways that Scholly could be relevant for subscribers at different age intervals as well—for high school and undergrad students, for grad school and PhD students, for parents of all these students, and for older students returning to college. We also had subscribers who were educators and college counselors looking for specific scholarships for their students.

For added value, we followed the Netflix model and added features such as our Scholly Editor, which helps subscribers check the spelling and grammar in their essays, and then we tried out a math app. We included testimonials from scholarship recipients who were our stars.

The stories of lives being changed with scholarship winnings sprinkled in at first and then came in by the boatloads. Everyone's story was different, but all shared the common theme of how empowering it was to embrace the very things that made them unique and find a scholarship designed for those attributes. Every report gave me the same thrill that I'd once experienced when I heard from the places where I'd applied myself. "Congratulations, we are pleased to inform you that you have been selected. . . ."

When the first waves of scholarship awards for Scholly users came through, I heard over and over how academic and professional dreams that once might have seemed too lofty were being made real. Students who were going to college for the first time or being able to continue working for their undergrad degree or receiving scholarships for an advanced grad degree were not just thanking Scholly but asking to be a part of our journey: they wanted to help get the word out on their own or even sign up to become a brand ambassador on our behalf.

Our subscribers and winners were as diverse as I could ever have imagined or planned. Let's not forget that there is financial need in every demographic, now more than ever.

It used to be that middle-class families could afford to send their kids to school. Rarely is that possible today without financial aid. Our outreach to new users was broad-based.

We teamed up with celebrities, casts of TV shows, Fortune 500 corporations, and iconic brands to create custom scholarships. We had drawing-style scholarships that required next to no application essay. We celebrated all of our milestones with our subscribers, without whom our success wouldn't have happened. At this writing, we are approximately 4 million strong and have helped users win over $100 million in scholarship awards. For a little over six years in existence, that is . . . incredible.

Whenever competitors knocked us—which happened regularly as other entities tried to get in on the outside scholarship search business—I had a "bring it on" response, telling my team not to sweat it, promising them that no one could claim the results that we did. The grumblings were evidence that we were killing it.

In late 2017, we became bicoastal, retaining our flagship office in Philly while moving most of our team, including me, to Los Angeles. In trying to be Netflix-like, I had also peered down the road and spotted a new phenomenon—a growing hub that merged tech with entertainment. In what was being called Silicon Beach, Los Angeles appeared to be at the exciting intersection of Hollywood, technology, and social entrepreneurship, and I thought we'd be well positioned to leverage the celebrities whose values aligned with ours.

Involving celebrities in your business or cause can be a slippery slope. You may get attention from having the support and excitement of a prominent name with millions of followers, but that doesn't necessarily translate to money or activism. We have found that exposure through press and media attention is much easier to monetize and actually moves the needle with subscriptions.

We have been fortunate, at the same time, to have attracted celebrities who are as engaged in our mission as we are. They have helped us build a platform that is fast becoming a movement. At the top of that list is Jesse Williams, star of *Grey's Anatomy*. The two of us met when we were at a TED conference in Vancouver, waiting in line for what I hoped was the bathroom.

Just being a fan, I began by complimenting him on his work and then added, "Do you know if this is the line to the men's bathroom?"

He laughed and said, "Better be. I've been here for ten minutes." Somehow that cracked me up to think we were both stuck in a line that might have not even been leading to the men's room. Eventually the line started to move, and sure enough, the bathroom came into sight.

On the way out, I had to acknowledge him for the speech he had recently given at the 2016 BET Awards after receiving an award for raising awareness of Black Lives Matter and in recognition of the documentary he had directed about the movement. I had been riveted and inspired by Jesse's oratory. He had said:

> Now, this award, this is not for me. This is for the real organizers all over the country. The activists, the civil rights attorneys, the struggling parents, the families, the teachers, the students that are realizing that a system built to divide and impoverish and destroy us cannot stand if we do. All right? It's kind of basic mathematics. The more we learn about who we are and how we got here, the more we will mobilize . . .
>
> Now, what we've been doing is looking at the data and we know that police somehow manage to deescalate, disarm, and not kill white people every day. So what's going to happen is we're going to have equal rights and justice in our own country or we will restructure their function in ours . . .
>
> Yesterday would have been young Tamir Rice's 14th birthday. So, I don't want to hear anymore about how far we've come when paid public servants can pull a drive-by on a 12-year-old playing alone in a park in broad daylight, killing him on television and then going home to make a sandwich. Tell Rekia Boyd how it's so much better to live in 2012, than it is to live in 1612 or

1712. Tell that to Eric Garner. Tell that to Sandra Bland. Tell that to Darrien Hunt.

Now, the thing is, though, all of us in here getting money, that alone isn't going to stop this. All right? Now dedicating our lives to getting money just to give it right back. For someone's brand on our body when we spent centuries praying with brands on our bodies and now we pray to get paid for brands on our bodies. There has been no war that we have not fought and died on the front lines of. There has been no job we haven't done. There's no tax they haven't levied against us. And we pay all of them. But freedom is somehow always conditional here. You're free, they keep telling us, but she would have been alive if she hadn't acted so free.

. . . The burden of the brutalized is not to comfort the bystander. That's not our job. . . . If you have a critique for the resistance, for our resistance, then you better have an established record of critique of our oppression. If you have no interest in equal rights for Black people, then do not make suggestions to those who do.

In light of the events of 2020 and the murders of George Floyd and Brianna Taylor by the police and more, Jesse's words were more than prophetic. Not stopping with police brutality and systemic racism in all of our systems, he went after his industry—Hollywood—and didn't mince any words:

> We've been floating this country on credit for centuries, yo. And we're done watching, and waiting while this invention called whiteness uses and abuses us. Burying Black people out of sight and out of mind, while extracting our culture, our dollars, our entertainment like oil—black gold. Ghettoizing and demeaning our creations then stealing them. Gentrifying our genius and then trying us on like costumes before discarding our bodies like rinds of strange fruit. The thing is that just because we're magic doesn't mean we're not real.

Jesse shook my hand and thanked me for acknowledging the speech. Then I went back to being a fan, and as we were both walking out, I had to ask, "Would you mind if I got a picture with you?"

Gracious and generous, Jesse replied, "Not at all." We took the shot, I thanked him, and then I honestly thought that would be the last time I saw him.

Then, as fate and Oprah (yes, Oprah is like fate) would have it, Jesse and I were both named to Oprah's Super Soul 100 list of her favorite people and invited to an Oprah Winfrey Network (OWN) brunch to meet Oprah and a small group of others who made the list.

Jesse and I started talking, and he told me that when we

last met he had actually recognized me from *Shark Tank*—and that he was a big fan of what I was doing with Scholly.

"You were a public high school teacher, right?"

Jesse nodded and then had a lot to say about the challenges facing college-bound students, as well as the need in our educational system for greater activism from all corners. Jesse had been quoted as saying, "We often grow up being told that we can do this or that, but if you don't see anybody that looks like you doing it, you don't believe you can do it." Because he had been fortunate to have great teachers (and parents who were great teachers), he had been inspired to be a great teacher. In addition to being an actor and, increasingly, an outspoken activist, Jesse had recently become an entrepreneur with the very cool app Ebroji, which he described as a different kind of curated approach to digital keyboards for finding the right GIF for every occasion.

We were clearly like-minded. Somehow I knew right away he would be an asset to helping get out the word about Scholly.

Initially, I went to him asking for a simple tweet about the company, but of course Jesse saw Scholly as something bigger, as a movement to change lives across America, and he wanted to be even more involved. As someone who had chosen to give voice to the many who had been silenced, Jesse let me know that for him Scholly was the natural next step.

We had ongoing conversations about the growing relevance of social entrepreneurs, particularly among Millennials. As we talked about my vision for Scholly being a movement to make education affordable for all and a springboard for raising the awareness needed to tackle the mounting problem of crippling student loan debt, he helped me see another strand to our brand story—the strand of Scholly as a Black-owned business.

Never before had I seen so clearly why forging our own paths and then leaving trails behind us mattered to all communities of color. In an economy that raises up Black-owned businesses and entrepreneurs who are BIPOC, LGBTQ+, and especially women, we have opportunity and economic mobility that alleviates poverty. Jesse helped me give voice to my feeling that too many Black people I hear feel there is no change until we infiltrate systems designed to misuse and exploit us. Why? I disagreed. My belief was that true change happens when we create systems to empower each other—so that we can take a seat at the tables we have built for ourselves.

To change problems like poverty and systemic racism, I pointed out, the person who has experienced the oppression can create real solutions. Later I posted in social media, "Let's create our own systems and rather than trying to beg for a seat at another man's table, let's take the time to build our own tables and let God prepare that table before our oppressors."

Jesse readily accepted our invitation for him to partner with Scholly as our chief brand ambassador and a board member. Since that time, he has continually looked for ways to leverage his platform as a means of introducing Scholly to even more students, helping them access even more funds for college.

Turning a brand into a movement is an exciting prospect that I first felt coming to life in February 2018 during the Scholly Summit in Chicago—which was also in the middle of one of the most volatile snowstorms in that city's recent history.

My executive team and I had flown from sunny Los Angeles the day before and landed in the bone-chilling cold of Chicago so we could host our first-ever scholarship summit. We'd arranged to bus more than a thousand high school students to an out-of-the-way venue for a cutting-edge, multimedia, no-expenses-spared conference designed to empower, enlighten, and educate—complete with a drawing for a $10,000 scholarship at the end of the day. The only requirement for students to enter the drawing was to show up at the summit. Our VIP speakers included activists, entrepreneurs, college recruiters, corporate executives, scholarship sponsors, philanthropists, former scholarship winners, recent college grads whose professional trajectories were already shaking up their respective fields, and high-profile celebrities.

Along with Jesse Williams the other main headliner was Chicago's own Chance the Rapper, our key sponsor, who had already donated over a million dollars to local public schools. When Chance first heard about Scholly, he generously purchased Scholly subscriptions for every eligible high school junior and senior in the entire city.

Actually, the concept for the summit had come about toward the last minute, when it became clear that we had no effective communication channels for reaching Chicago's public high school students. I mean, what good is a free app that helps you apply for scholarships so you can afford college (or any kind of tool for that matter!) if you don't know what it can do for you and how to use it? So instead of trying to beam our program electronically into classrooms—which was opposed by school administrators—I decided to go another route. Rather than marshaling our troops and going into students' usual environment, why not get the students out of the classroom and into a setting that could be fun and inspiring? Administrators pushed back, saying they didn't want students to miss a day of school, so we set the date for February 10—a Saturday.

Nothing along these lines had ever been tried—not for any major municipal public school system and certainly not by us. However, as the planning pieces fell into place, our efforts galvanized attention. Our brand partners came to us, asking, "How can we help?" Next thing we knew, we were bombarded with requests for press credentials by every major media outlet.

The scope of the summit kept growing—along with the budget. Every time a guest speaker jumped on board, we had to coordinate that many more details. We're talking about flights, hotels, and the speaker's involvement in the program and in other gatherings before and after. My chief of staff, working from our original Philadelphia office, had convinced me early in the process to bring in an event planner from Toronto. She did a phenomenal job working with our two offices (LA and Philly) and with the various vendors in Chicago.

Everything was going so perfectly that I made the mistake of congratulating myself and my team for our fantastic planning. We relaxed and figured everything was ready to go smoothly.

That is, until February hit and the weather in Chicago went all to hell. Out of nowhere, the snow began on February 3 and would not stop for nine straight days. The snow fell and fell and fell, tying records that had been set once in 2009 and before that in 1902. And that's what we flew into.

On the night before the summit, the team and I huddled in my hotel room and faced the reality that half of our attendees might not make it. I took in everyone's stressed-out faces, and it was then that I spoke to the challenge of the moment and let them know, "Look, we can only control the things we can control."

Now it was up to me to make the most of the things that could go right and that were within our control. My pep talk was intended as much to rouse my own spirits as it was to remind the team that this was all upside. We were here to do some good, to inspire Chicago's high school students not only to dream differently about their own possibilities but also to see that there was support they might never have known about.

"The show must go on," I quipped, laughing, because how much more old-school can you get than that? Still, we all vowed to give it our all, no matter how many showed up. We were going to learn a lot and make the next summit even better.

We high-fived, we hugged, and then I shooed everyone out, saying, "Y'all better get some sleep."

After going over a few more particulars that couldn't wait until the morning, I stayed up, making notes and plotting out different scenarios and contingencies. I had to chuckle, remembering when I was a kid and how much time I used to spend playing video games that required you to outsmart your unpredictable opponent. And here we were.

When I hit the hotel breakfast table the next morning, my team tried hard to hide their grim faces. Several flights had been grounded. Several more were in a holding pattern. Media reps had begun calling to ask if we were going to cancel.

"No, we're going ahead as planned," I shrugged, way too cheery for the others. "It's gonna be great, even if it's us alone talking about the importance of college and the app. The people who need to get here will be here."

Everyone nodded, going along with me.

"Besides," I reminded them, "we have a DJ and he's local."

I had a point. Chance the Rapper had arranged for his own DJ to help set the mood for the students. My optimism apparently did the trick, and everyone powered up on breakfast before we dashed into the cold and snow to catch the van that would take us to the venue—a massive indoor tennis pavilion.

Once there, we spread out, welcoming the out-of-towners who had begun to show. Nobody chose to throw in the towel. They'd traveled through a blizzard to get here. The buzz and the excitement were real.

"What Snowpocalypse?" joked one of my friends, head of a nonprofit in DC. Outside in a 2018 world of climate change and escalating income injustice, it was brutal, but in here where it was warm and hopeful and game-changing, all systems were go.

We pushed back our start time, attempting to accommodate late arrivals at the airport. The DJ sent word that he was going to be late. Then the driver bringing in Jesse went to the wrong address. By then, some of our VIPs and sponsors were starting to get restless. Thinking fast, I decided to improvise and turn the backstage greenroom into a networking event.

In the middle of introducing a couple of tech folks, I was signaled by a member of my LA team who was in charge of coordinating with the charter buses we'd hired to bring in the students. She had a panic-stricken expression on her face.

I hurried over, and she leaned in to tell me that after being notified that the school buses were en route and should be arriving any minute, the dispatcher alerted her to a problem.

"What?"

"They lost a bus." She paused, then continued. "They can't find it. They lost a bus and don't know where it is." In other words, forty students and a bus driver had gone missing in the Snowpocalypse.

My inner voice threw a fit: *Are you kidding me? We're short a bus?! We lost forty high school students because we dragged them out in a blizzard?*

Rather than say any of that, or worse, I nodded and calmly asked her to get me the dispatcher on the phone. In problem-solving mode, I realized that if the bus had broken down somewhere, we could send out a fleet of Uber drivers we'd already contracted.

The dispatcher connected me to his boss, who was

apologetic and promised to coordinate with law enforcement to scour the city and find the missing bus. It was
then—as I turned to my chief of staff and told him the latest, asking to have the recently arrived DJ get going with
music as the thousand-plus students began to trickle in—
that I realized somebody somewhere had bet some money
on us not pulling this off.

That wasn't going to happen, not on my watch. This was,
after all, my game—and I controlled what I could control.
We were going to make history this day.

With that, I heard the voice of my event planner telling me that the missing bus had arrived. Where had they
been? Something about someone having to go to the bathroom? After that, I can honestly report the event was as
close to seamless as I could have ever dreamed. Chance
the Rapper and Jesse Williams took us to church, energiz-
ing the thousand-plus high school students with reminders
that there were teachers, mentors, entrepreneurs, colleges,
brands, and business companies who were there to help
them succeed, and that at no time in their lives would there
be so much help available as there was at this juncture of
their lives . . . and not to take it for granted.

The chemistry was off the charts with so many different
problem-solvers coming together on issues of poverty, lack
of access to money for education, and how to create more
bridges into successful careers after college or alternative
training programs.

The day culminated, as planned, with the drawing for a $10,000 Scholly scholarship that we provided. Again, any student who had signed up with the app and who showed up in person was eligible to win. For the winner, Alexiea Feaster, a senior at Chicago's William J. Bogan High School whose dream was to go to medical school, the scholarship from us was a vote of confidence that brought her one step closer to being able to afford to attend Xavier University of Louisiana. Blogging for us, she noted that the summit was a chance for her to give shape to her goal to one day "save lives for those who are hurting and helpless." One of the messages she took away from the remarks of one panelist was that going to college to pursue your ambitions is bigger than just you. She described what that meant to her:

Life will bring us trauma, failure, and obstacles, but all of that is part of a much bigger picture of our success. We cannot get caught up in these micro-moments and let negativity bring us down. Most importantly, we need to accept help earlier on in order to make the journey to success an easier one and pass that knowledge on to others. When he said this, I felt inspired, motivated, and understood my purpose. I know that to achieve greatness I will have to think about the lives of others because how can an economy flourish if no one can pass knowledge on to the next person? Thank you, Scholly, for granting me this scholarship and opportunity. You have opened the doors to success for me and I hope I can continue to make you proud!

The day was perfect. We danced our way out into the snowstorm—which had miraculously stopped—with ambitious plans to expand Scholly's future summit dreams. What if, for example, before students even applied to college, there was a national summit like a massive college fair, with planning workshops to help every student plan for how they were going to pay for their undergraduate years and beyond? How could we pull off something like that? It had never been done before but . . . wait, isn't that the point?

It seemed like a lifetime ago that I fended off homelessness and worried that I would never get off the island and that there wouldn't be money to go to college. And there I'd been, up onstage with Chance the Rapper and Jesse Williams talking about the vast amount of opportunity for those willing to go in search of it. The moment was another turning point for me that gave birth to ideas for similar events with other partnerships. *Forbes* sponsored a Harlem Scholly Summit that included subscriptions it purchased for all college-bound Harlem high school students. A Los Angeles Summit was soon in the works, along with plans for Miami, Seattle, and other cities. In the lead-up to the Los Angeles event, we forged an exciting alliance with Will Smith and Jada Pinkett Smith to fund scholarships for students seeking education and opportunities in the entertainment field.

In 2019 I had an epiphany about a new way to fix the system and build our own tables of opportunity. Just as I had thought, years earlier, that the system for finding money for college was dysfunctional, I was overwhelmed by the sob stories I heard from students dealing with debt. Rather than bemoaning how it had gotten out of hand, I declared out loud one afternoon, "There's got to be a better way."

Then an idea hit me so hard I could have fallen over. Why couldn't we approach our brand partners to develop and offer scholarships earmarked for reducing and erasing student debt? Why couldn't we give away weekly checks from drawings rather than requiring scholarship essays?

In the two years that followed, we began to implement some of those debt reduction strategies and pulled off goals for more summits and other ambitious undertakings. We filled university stadiums and continued to push the envelope. Our subscriber base nearly doubled. From what didn't work, we learned valuable lessons, and from what did work, we applied the knowledge gained to keep the momentum going. We included other, value-added software and services to inspire and assist in scholarship essay writing. We also diversified by teaming up with sponsors to create scholarships—going much further off our main path of helping subscribers search for existing scholarships. We lobbied Congress on behalf of students, families, and educational institutions to address lack of access to funding; we audaciously started creating partnerships in the private sector to offer scholarships for directly erasing debts.

In 2019 we road tested new features and some of our loan payoff scholarships, but it was in 2020 that we pulled out the stops. In the middle of a brutal pandemic that was disproportionately killing people of color, a political landscape during an election year that looked like the days right before the Civil War, and a long overdue reckoning by protesters against police brutality and systemic racism—millions from all backgrounds took to the streets in the largest civil rights movement ever assembled—we changed the game by connecting private and public entities on paying for college and erasing debt. When college campuses shut down in the spring of 2020, we also were able to give emergency funds to students who could not afford alternative housing, and, in some cases, to their families.

Some of the most encouraging signs I saw during the largely peaceful protests were the coming together of diverse groups that wanted to engage in dialogue, a vast concerted effort to support Black lives and Black-owned businesses, and a new commitment by people who are not of color to read and become better informed about how to be allies in the struggle for economic and political justice and equality.

The takeaway for me was that the next chapter in my journey may be doing more to create access to investment and opportunity leading to business ownership for African-American entrepreneurs and women and for members of other communities left out or ignored. When you go where the path does not lead, you never know how it will all play out.

It seems to me that this inflection point in history is a Call to Action to all of us. We don't have a choice as to where we're going—but we must go. We must change the game to make it fairer and more just in every way. *We* can pursue paths in business, in service, as change agents, or as all of that.

My story, though unique, is universal. My hope is that it has shown you what's possible and even perhaps necessary. It's a metaphor for the journeys that so many are taking in the current climate of uncertainty, a time when so many proven paths of the past are starting to become obsolete. We are all forging a new path that doesn't yet exist. This is our time to write a new chapter for every generation—one of redemption and empowerment, of hope and opportunity for all.

Acknowledgments

When I first started to write the book that became *Go Where There Is No Path*, I quickly realized that this was one path I was not about to forge on my own. Not only had I never written a book before, but the process wasn't something I'd studied closely. What I did know was that I genuinely wanted to tell my story as a social entrepreneur in a way that could make a real difference in other people's lives. To that end, I was truly fortunate to meet the best possible guides along that path. I am forever thankful to everyone who has played a meaningful role in helping me bring my vision to life.

At the top of that list, I am indebted to literary agent Mollie Glick who believed in me and this book before it existed on paper. Thank you to Mollie and everyone at CAA for your support of me and passion for this project. Mollie, thank you as well for your recommendation of coauthor Mim Eichler Rivas. I couldn't have asked for a better collaborator than Mim—who worked with me tirelessly to help me tell my story in the most compelling way possible. I appreciate her experience and insight in helping structure and shape this book in a way that gives actionable steps to those trying to go where there is no path.

I am most grateful to have found the ideal publishing home at William Morrow/HarperCollins. Thank you to Mauro DiPreto, senior vice president and executive editor, for shepherding this book along at every stage, for your editorial guidance, and especially for asking all the right questions early on. Our sincere thanks go to assistant editor Vedika Khanna for making sure we met our production deadlines, and more. Further gratitude extends to the entire William Morrow/HarperCollins team—Liate Stehlik, Benjamin Steinberg, Kayleigh George, Christina Joell, Pamela Barricklow, Elizabeth Blaise, Evangelos Vasilakis, Aryana Hendrawan, Elina Cohen, Victor Hendrickson, and Ploy Siripant.

Special thanks to Chris Gardner, Jesse Williams, Lori Greiner, and Daymond John for your belief in Scholly and giving this book your kind words of support. I must acknowledge the entire Scholly team for going with me off the beaten track and helping to leave a trail. I could not be prouder of what we have accomplished in so short an amount of time.

Scholly would not have come so far or so fast without the help of three individuals in particular—Josh Koppelman,

Chuck Sacco, and Steve Case. Thank you to all of you in Dorm Room Fund, to my peers and professors at Drexel University, and to the city of Philadelphia. My first home away from home proved to be a powerful launch pad.

I want to acknowledge the cities, states, and educational institutions that have purchased subscriptions for whole student bodies in your jurisdictions. I also want to say an overdue thanks to every sponsor of every scholarship, large and small, who have directly benefitted Scholly subscribers and others who would not have been able to afford higher education otherwise. Likewise, I am encouraged and inspired by many who are now providing scholarships to pay off student debt. Most of all, I want to thank our Scholly community of subscribers and users for sharing your successes with us and with others. I encourage readers of all ages and stages, to join our family at myscholly.com. Check out our book page and important news and offers as new opportunities arise.

Finally, I want to heartily acknowledge and thank my early champions—Dr. Karen Starks, Ms. Tara Tidwell, and Thelma Gray, my late great-grandmother.

Author's Note

The personal stories that I have shared in recalling my journey as a social entrepreneur include remembered conversations and descriptions of encounters with others that are not meant to be word-for-word reenactments. Even so, I'm confident that I've retold these conversations in the spirit of the words with which they were spoken.